THE LUCENT LIBRARY OF SCIENCE AND TECHNOLOGY

Comets and Asteroids

by Don Nardo

LUCENT
BOOKS®

THOMSON

GALE

San Diego • Detroit • New York • San Francisco • Cleveland • New Haven, Conn. • Waterville, Maine • London • Munich

Cover: Comet Hyakutake, discovered in 1996, is one of the brightest comets ever discovered, and has a tail more than 300 million miles long.

LIBRARY OF CONGRESS CATALOGING-IN-PUBLICATION DATA

Nardo, Don, 1947–
    Comets and asteroids / by Don Nardo.
        v. cm. — (The Lucent library of science and technology)
Includes bibliographical references.
Contents: Comets demystified, asteroids discovered—How asteroids and comets formed—Vital statistics of asteroids and comets—Voyages to the comets and asteroids—How humans will mine asteroids and comets—When comets and asteroids strike earth.
        ISBN 1-59018-286-3 (hardback : alk. paper)
        1. Comets—Juvenile literature. 2. Asteroids—Juvenile literature. [1. Comets. 2. Asteroids.] I. Title. II. Series.
        QB721.5N37 2004
        523.6—dc22
                                                                        2003016736

Printed in the United States of America

Table of Contents

Foreword

"The world has changed far more in the past 100 years than in any other century in history. The reason is not political or economic, but technological—technologies that flowed directly from advances in basic science."

— Stephen Hawking, "A Brief History of Relativity," *Time,* 2000

The twentieth-century scientific and technological revolution that British physicist Stephen Hawking describes in the above quote has transformed virtually every aspect of human life at an unprecedented pace. Inventions unimaginable a century ago have not only become commonplace but are now considered necessities of daily life. As science historian James Burke writes, "We live surrounded by objects and systems that we take for granted, but which profoundly affect the way we behave, think, work, play, and in general conduct our lives."

For example, in just one hundred years, transportation systems have dramatically changed. In 1900 the first gasoline-powered motorcar had just been introduced, and only 144 miles of U.S. roads were hard-surfaced. Horse-drawn trolleys still filled the streets of American cities. The airplane had yet to be invented. Today 217 million vehicles speed along 4 million miles of U.S. roads. Humans have flown to the moon and commercial aircraft are capable of transporting passengers across the Atlantic Ocean in less than three hours.

The transformation of communications has been just as dramatic. In 1900 most Americans lived and worked on farms without electricity or mail delivery. Few people had ever heard a radio or spoken on a telephone. A hundred years later, 98 percent of American homes have telephones and televisions and more than 50 percent have personal computers. Some families even have more than one television and computer, and cell phones are now commonplace, even among the young. Data beamed from communication satellites routinely predict global weather conditions and fiber-optic cable, e-mail, and the Internet have made worldwide telecommunication instantaneous.

Perhaps the most striking measure of scientific and technological change can be seen in medicine and public health. At the beginning of the twentieth century, the average American life span was forty-seven years. By the end of the century the average life span was approaching eighty years, thanks to advances in medicine including the development of vaccines and antibiotics, the discovery of powerful diagnostic tools such as X rays, the life-saving technology of cardiac and neonatal care, and improvements in nutrition and the control of infectious disease.

Rapid change is likely to continue throughout the twenty-first century as science reveals more about physical and biological processes such as global warming, viral replication, and electrical conductivity, and as people apply that new knowledge to personal decisions and government policy. Already, for example, an international treaty calls for immediate reductions in industrial and automobile emissions in response to studies that show a potentially dangerous rise in global temperatures is caused by human activity. Taking an active role in determining the direction of future changes depends on education; people must understand the possible uses of scientific research and the effects of the technology that surrounds them.

The Lucent Books Library of Science and Technology profiles key innovations and discoveries that have transformed the modern world. Each title strives to make a complex scientific discovery, technology, or phenomenon understandable and relevant to the reader. Because scientific discovery is rarely straightforward, each title explains the dead ends, fortunate accidents, and basic scientific methods by which the research into the subject proceeded. And every book examines the practical applications of an invention, branch of science, or scientific principle in industry, public health, and personal life, as well as potential future uses and effects based on ongoing research. Fully documented quotations, annotated bibliographies that include both print and electronic sources, glossaries, indexes, and technical illustrations are among the supplemental features designed to point researchers to further exploration of the subject.

Introduction

Mountains in the Sky

If a person goes outside on a clear, moonless night in the countryside, far from city lights, he or she will be treated to a breathtaking sight. Above stretches a velvet black canopy studded with thousands of pinpoints of light, some bright and lustrous, others so faint they are barely visible. Most of these, of course, are stars like the Sun, except that they lie much farther away than the huge gaseous ball whose light and heat make life on Earth possible.

A few of the brighter points of light in the dark canopy are planets in our own solar system, the Sun's family. But these few easily visible solid bodies, each thousands of miles in diameter, are only the tip of the iceberg, so to speak, of the material making up the solar system. Lurking in the darkness among them, usually invisible to unaided human eyes, are billions of smaller objects. Some are no larger than cars or houses, while others are five, ten, fifty, or a hundred miles across. "Lost amid the stars," writes noted science historian Curtis Peebles, "there are mountains in the sky. Some are worlds in their own right, others are the irregular splinters of collisions [that happened] ages ago."[1]

Those orbiting mountains that are composed mainly of metal and rock are known as asteroids, while those made up mostly of ice and rock are comets. Because of their relatively small size (as compared to planets and stars), most asteroids and comets are difficult to see without the use of a large telescope; however, on occasion a comet will grow a tail and pass near enough to Earth to become visible to the naked eye.

Disaster and the Deaths of Princes

For these reasons, no one knew about the existence of asteroids until modern times, when large telescopes became common. In contrast, people have seen comets since ancient times, indeed since modern humans first appeared on Earth more than a hundred thousand years ago. Over the centuries, various peoples assigned names to these objects, and because comets have such a distinct look—like fuzzy stars with cloudlike tails—most of the names are similar to one another. The ancient Chinese called them "broom stars," for example. The Aztecs, who dwelled in what is now Mexico, called them "smok-

Comet Hale-Bopp, discovered in July 1995. Humans have observed comets for thousands of years but have only recently uncovered their true nature.

ing stars," while in ancient Zaire (in Africa), they were "hair stars," in reference to their hairlike tails. Similarly, the European name—comet—which became universally accepted, comes from the ancient Greek word *kome*, meaning "hair."

Whatever the ancients chose to call comets, nearly all agreed that these objects were omens, or supernatural signs, of one kind or another. The most common view was that they foretold coming disasters or ill fortune. An ancient Chinese document titled *Record of the World's Change* states:

> Comets are vile stars. Every time they appear in the south, something happens to wipe out the old and establish the new. Also, when comets appear, whales die. In Sung . . . times, when a comet appeared in the constellation of the Big Dipper, all soldiers died in chaos. . . . When a comet appears in the North Star, the emperor is replaced. If it appears in the end of the Big Dipper, everywhere there are uprisings and war continues for several years. If it appears in the bowl of the Dipper, a prince controls the emperor. Gold and gems become worthless. . . . Scoundrels harm nobles. Some leaders appear, causing disturbances. Ministers conspire to rebel against the emperor.[2]

The other common belief regarding cometary omens was that they signaled the birth, death, or military victories of great kings, generals, and other human leaders. The immortal English playwright William Shakespeare summarized it best in a famous line from his play *Julius Caesar:* "When beggars die, there are no comets seen; the heavens themselves blaze forth the death of princes."[3] In fact, the passing of the real Julius Caesar, some sixteen centuries before Shakespeare wrote these lines, was said to have been marked by a comet. According to Caesar's Greek biographer Plutarch: "Of [the] supernatural events [marking Caesar's death] there was, first, the great comet which shone very brightly for seven nights after Caesar's murder and then disappeared."[4] Similarly, in Plutarch's own time, a comet that became visible in A.D. 79 was widely believed to be associated with the death of the Roman emperor Vespasian. (The idea that comets were harbingers of disaster was still commonplace; in A.D. 66, a bright comet was seen as an omen of the destruction of the city of Jerusalem that year by the Romans.)

The Voice of Reason Ignored

Not all of the ancients were convinced that comets were completely supernatural, however. The Greek philosopher-scientist Democritus (born in 460 B.C.) was the first known person to suggest that these celestial objects might have natural origins. He proposed that comets existed among the distant stars and planets and formed when one of these bodies came too near another. In the following century, the more influential Greek thinker Aristotle disagreed. In his view, comets were natural, but they existed inside Earth's own atmosphere—the result of hot, dry gases seeping out of the ground and igniting high in the air.

A few centuries later, the Roman playwright and thinker Seneca the Younger declared that Aristotle was wrong. In a treatise titled *On Comets*, the seventh book of a larger work, the *Natural Questions*, Seneca argued that comets could not be moving through the atmosphere. If they were, he said, the wind should disturb their movements, yet even after a sudden storm a comet stayed on its stately path. Seneca was not exactly sure what comets were. But he had the humility to admit it and the foresight to predict that future scientists would discover the truth. "The day will come," he wrote,

> when the progress of research through long ages will reveal to sight the mysteries of nature that are now concealed. A single lifetime, though it were wholly devoted to the study of the sky, does not

This drawing of Democritus, the first scientist to suggest comets are natural objects, is fanciful. No one knows his actual appearance.

suffice for the investigation of problems of such complexity. . . . It must, therefore, require long successive ages to unfold all. The day will yet come when posterity [future generations] will be amazed that we remained ignorant of things that will to them seem so plain. . . . The man will come one day who will explain in what regions the comets move, why they diverge so much from the other stars, what is their size and their nature. Many discoveries are reserved for the ages still to be when our memory shall have perished. . . . Nature does not reveal all her secrets at once.[5]

Seneca's voice of reason regarding comets and other aspects of the heavens had little or no effect on the thinking of later generations. In medieval times, the ancient superstitions about comets continued to prevail. In the seventh century, Isidor, Bishop of Seville, an influential Christian historian, declared that comets foreshadow wars and disease epidemics. And the fact that from time to time comets did materialize during wars was enough to convince most people that the bishop must be right.

In 1066, for instance, a bright comet appeared just as William the Conqueror was invading England. The common belief at the time was that this apparition was an evil omen for England's King Harold, and indeed, Harold soon went down to defeat, initiating the Norman occupation of the country. (The well-known Bayeux Tapestry, celebrating the Norman victory, shows the comet, which modern scientists now agree is the famous Halley's comet in one of its many periodic visits to Earth's neighborhood.)

This section of the Bayeux Tapestry shows Comet Halley in the sky (upper left), an evil omen for England's King Harold.

Incredibly, a certain degree of fear and awe of comets continued into modern times, even after science showed conclusively that these objects are simply stray chunks of ice and rock roaming the solar system. When Comet Biela passed close to Earth in 1892, for example, terror gripped many people across the globe. Typical of the reactions were those reported in an Atlanta, Georgia, newspaper:

Life's building blocks may have come to Earth on comets and asteroids, as shown in this imaginative sketch of bacteria riding an asteroid.

> The fear which took possession of many citizens has not yet abated. The general expectation hereabouts was that the comet would be heard from on Saturday night. As one result, the confessionals of the two Catholic churches here were crowded yesterday evening. As the night advanced, there were many who insisted that they could detect changes in the atmosphere. The air, they said, was stifling. . . . Tonight (Saturday) they [the churches] are all full, and sermons suited to the terrible occasion are being delivered.[6]

Cosmic Connections to Humans?

Today, by contrast, astronomers and other scientists view comets and their cosmic cousins, asteroids, as more fascinating than frightening and find that much can be learned from studying them. Both of these classes of celestial bodies have been around for billions of years. So they offer important clues to conditions in the solar system during its early years.

In addition, comets and the materials composing them may well have crucial connections to human beings and other life on Earth. "Comets are the least understood objects in the solar system," says NASA comet expert Donald Yeomans. "And they're probably the most important when it comes to you and me."[7] Yeomans is referring to the current theory that much of the water on Earth was delivered by infalling comets, as well as another hypothesis that organic compounds in comets brought the precursors of life to our planet.

The very fact that comets, and asteroids too, do occasionally fall to Earth is another reason that these bodies are important to humans. Nearly all scientists now accept that the impact of a comet or asteroid wiped out more than half the animal species on the planet, including the dinosaurs, 65 million years ago. Such disasters can and will happen again in the future. Ironically, therefore, ancient fears of these objects were not totally misplaced, even if the reasons given in those days were wrong. What is certain is that the more we study and understand these bodies, the better chance we have of controlling them and keeping them from wiping out human civilization. After all, it is and always will remain in the best interest of everyone for the millions of mountains that hurtle through the sky to stay in their own domain.

Chapter 1

Comets Demystified, Asteroids Discovered

Until the emergence of modern astronomy in the 1500s and 1600s, comets remained mysterious and frightening signs of disastrous or extraordinary events. The noted Protestant leader Martin Luther, who died in 1546, stated the common view. He was aware of the writings of Greeks like Aristotle and Romans like Seneca, who had held that comets result from natural processes. Luther flat out rejected the ideas of these "heathens," or nonbelievers in Christianity, saying, "The heathen writes that the comet may arise from natural causes; but God creates not one [comet] that does not foretoken a sure calamity."[8]

In the two centuries following Luther's passing, however, a number of pioneering astronomers demonstrated that comets are indeed natural, rather than supernatural, bodies. Moreover, these scientists showed, comets orbit the sun. And following their measurable, predictable orbits, some comets return to Earth's neighborhood on a regular basis. In this way, even though astronomers were still unsure of the exact origins, size, and composition of comets, they managed to demystify largely these traditional harbingers of doom.

The discovery of asteroids, celestial bodies that are closely related to comets, soon followed. Only forty-three years after the first confirmed return of a periodic comet in 1758, an astronomer sighted the largest asteroid in the solar system. At the time, scientists thought this object was a small planet. And for a while, as other large asteroids were discovered, these bodies were routinely called "minor planets." Eventually, though, it became clear that they represented an entirely new class of celestial bodies—hunks of rock and metal wandering through the dark gulfs of the solar system along with the comets.

Tycho Measures a Comet

One major difference in early views of these objects was that astronomers recognized from the beginning that asteroids lie well beyond Earth in outer space; by contrast, even as late as Martin Luther's time, most people still assumed that comets moved within Earth's atmosphere, where they believed God had placed them. This antiquated view of comets was about to change, however. In 1546, the year Luther died, a boy named Tycho Brahe was born in Denmark. A brilliant individual, Tycho, as everyone called him, grew up to be an astronomer with his own observatory. He had al-

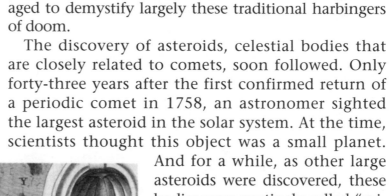

An engraving shows Tycho Brahe, who proved that comets lie beyond Earth's atmosphere.

ready made a name for himself in scientific circles
when a bright comet appeared in 1577. Tycho suspected that comets were physical objects existing
millions of miles from Earth. And because the new
comet was slow moving and stayed in the sky for
months, he had an opportunity to study it carefully
and test this theory.

Tycho was able to prove that the comet was far away
using a simple but ingenious technique. According to
noted astronomer Carl Sagan and his colleague Ann
Druyan:

> Tycho asked himself how the comet would look if
> it were merely an atmospheric disturbance and
> close to the Earth, and also how it would look if it
> were a body like the planets or the stars, far from
> the Earth. He was able to hold two contradictory
> ideas in his head at the same time. Place your fin-
> ger in front of your nose and alternately wink your
> left and right eyes. You will see the finger seem to
> move against the more distant landscape. Now
> move the finger to arm's length and wink again.
> The finger still moves, but less so. The apparent
> motion is called parallax; it is merely the change
> in perspective from left eye to right. . . . Tycho real-
> ized that this same principle can be applied to a
> comet—provided you could observe it from two
> widely separated observatories. If the comet is
> close to the Earth, the perspective will change
> greatly between the two observatories. . . . But if
> the comet is far from the Earth, then both observa-
> tories will see the comet in front of the same con-
> stellation.[9]

Tycho correctly reasoned that if the comet was in
Earth's atmosphere, it would be close enough to observers to cause a large parallax. Yet he could detect
almost no parallax at all. Thus, he concluded, the
comet must be located well beyond the Moon.
Furthermore, Tycho said, if comets move among the

distant planets, they must be natural celestial bodies, and thus there is little to fear from them.

Edmond Halley's Triumph

Tycho had taken an important step toward eliminating the mystery surrounding comets. But he was not fated to be the man whom Seneca had fifteen centuries earlier predicted would one day explain how comets move. That major comet pioneer turned out to be English astronomer Edmond Halley, who was born near London in 1656.

In 1680, after establishing himself as a brainy, eager researcher, Halley began to acquire an intense interest in comets. That was the year that a particularly bright comet was seen in European skies. Halley was aboard a ferry on his way to France when he first saw the object, and after landing he went directly to the Paris Observatory to discuss the apparition with the facility's director, Jean-Dominique Cassini. The meeting proved important because Cassini revealed to Halley an unprecedented theory about the new comet. Cassini suspected that this object was the very same comet that Tycho had measured in 1577. This suggested that, like a planet, the comet was moving in a regular orbit around the sun and making repeated visits to Earth's vicinity.

Halley was intrigued. Two years later, another bright comet appeared, an object that was to prove crucial to both scientific understanding of comets and Halley's reputation. Over time, Halley studied the comet, along with all known data on sightings and attempted measurements of past comets. And he became convinced that at least some of these bodies moved in long, oval-shaped orbits around the sun. "The space between the sun and the fixed stars is so immense," he declared, "that there is room enough for a comet to revolve, though the period of its revolution [around the sun must] be vastly long."[10]

In 1695 Halley announced that he had determined the orbit of the comet of 1682. Moreover, he said, this comet seemed to follow the very same path that the bright comets of 1531 and 1607 had, which had convinced him that all the objects were one and the same. The comet must have an orbital period of approximately seventy-six years, Halley said, and would surely return again. "If according to what we have already said, it should return again about the year 1758,"[11] he stated.

Edmond Halley determined that the orbit of the comet of 1682 matched those of two previous comets. He suggested all three were the same object.

Sadly, Halley died in 1742, just a few years before the highly anticipated return of his comet. Some scientists doubted that he had been right. But sure enough, the object appeared at the precise time and in the same area of the sky that Halley had predicted. On Christmas night in 1758, a German amateur astronomer named Johann Palitzsch was the first person to catch sight of the comet. (Subsequent studies indicated that the Chinese had observed it in 240 B.C. and various Europeans in A.D. 684, 1066, and 1301.) Halley's scientific triumph had shown conclusively that comets and other heavenly bodies are not divine signs and portents but physical, measurable objects following natural laws.

A Suspicious Planetary Pattern

Unlike Edmond Halley and other scientists who searched for periodic comets, astronomers in the late

1700s were not systematically looking for asteroids. Indeed, they still had no notion of the existence of such bodies. The big astronomy news in the era immediately following the 1758 return of Halley's comet was astronomer William Herschel's discovery of Uranus, the seventh known planet in the solar system. (The others were Mercury, Venus, Earth, Mars, Jupiter, and Saturn.)

Though finding Uranus, which orbits far beyond Saturn, greatly increased the apparent size of the solar system, most astronomers felt that the Sun's family was still incomplete. This view derived from the

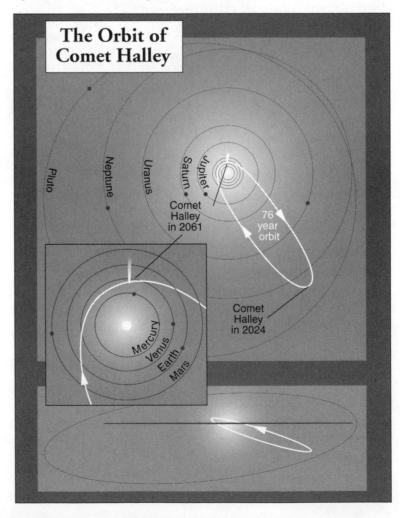

The Orbit of Comet Halley

Pluto

Neptune

Uranus

Saturn

Jupiter

Comet Halley in 2061

76 year orbit

Comet Halley in 2024

Mercury

Venus

Earth

Mars

manner in which the orbits of the known planets were spaced in relation to the Sun. Each successive planet was situated about one-and-a-half to two times as far from the sun as the one before it.

The first astronomer to notice this suspicious mathematical pattern was a German named Johann Titius. In 1772, nine years before the discovery of Uranus, he wrote, "Divide the distance from the sun to Saturn into 100 parts; then Mercury is separated by 4 such parts from the sun; Venus by $4 + 3 = 7$ such parts; the Earth by $4 + 6 = 10$; Mars by $4 + 12 = 16$." The trouble was that, although the six planets then known followed the pattern fairly well, a gap existed between the orbits of Mars and Jupiter. "After Mars," Titius pointed out, "there follows a distance of $4 + 24 = 28$ parts, but so far no planet or satellite has been sighted there."[12]

The same year that Titius called attention to this mathematical planetary pattern and its strange omission, another German astronomer, Johann Bode, mentioned it in a new book. For reasons unknown, Bode did not credit Titius as the discoverer of the planetary pattern. So Titius's contribution was temporarily overlooked, and astronomers began referring to the pattern as Bode's Law. Fortunately for Titius, Bode later admitted his error and the pattern came to be called the Titius-Bode Law.

Herschel's discovery of Uranus seemed to confirm the Titius-Bode pattern. Titius's mathematical scheme predicted a trans-Saturnian planet at a distance of $4 + 192 = 196$ parts. And actual measurements gave Uranus's distance a value of 192 parts, close enough to prove that a real planetary pattern did exist.

Found, Lost, and Found Again

Why, then, had no new planet been discovered between Mars and Jupiter, where the Titius-Bode Law indicated there should be one? Most astronomers

A Comet Hunter Strikes Ice

Professional astronomers are not the only ones who discover comets. In fact, many of these celestial bodies are found each year by dedicated amateurs using small telescopes. In this excerpt from an article in the January 2003 issue of *Astronomy,* aerospace engineer Tom Polakis recalls a moment of success for one persistent amateur astronomer.

Some comet hunters find success only after a lifetime of effort. Patrick Stonehouse had searched in vain for comets for several hundred hours over 30 years. Then, on April 22, 1998, he struck ice. Beginning his first comet sweep of the night with his 17.5-inch scope, Stonehouse immediately noticed a suspicious object. Over 20 minutes, the object moved northwest. The next two nights were clear; the comet was confirmed on April 25, and named C/1998 H1. . . . Stonehouse fondly recalls those intervening days as filled with both sleep deprivation and excitement. Today, Stonehouse sweeps for comets with a 25-inch telescope. He hopes to find another comet or asteroid, but if not, he says, "I see a multitude of diverse and magnificent heavenly objects during every search, so I am always happy in the searching and never feel disappointed for not having found anything new."

came to believe that such a planet must exist. Somehow, they assumed, it had thus far escaped detection, but they were sure the situation could be remedied by a large-scale systematic search. Accordingly, in 1800 a group of German astronomers organized by Franz Xaver von Zach met and mapped out such a search. Calling themselves the "Celestial Police," they sent invitations to join in the search to scientists across Europe.

One of the men Zach recruited for this concerted effort to find the missing planet was an Italian monk and astronomer named Giuseppe Piazzi, director of the Palermo Observatory. On January 1, 1801, Piazzi concentrated his attention on part of the constellation Taurus, the bull. It was not long before he noticed a dim star that did not appear on the standard sky chart he was using. Piazzi realized that the object could be a previously uncharted comet. Yet he also suspected, and sincerely hoped, that the intruder in Taurus might be the missing planet needed to fill the gap in the Titius-Bode Law.

To make sure the object was moving, as planets do, Piazzi observed it on the following night. He found to his delight that it had indeed shifted its position in relation to the fixed background stars. Between January 3 and February 11, Piazzi made twenty more observations of the mysterious object before it moved behind the sun. Although he was excited about the possibility that he had discovered an eighth planet, like a good

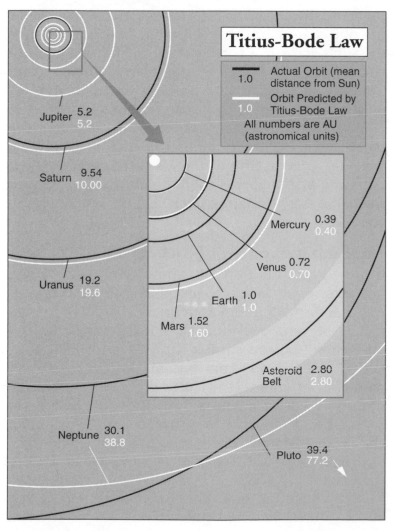

Titius-Bode Law

1.0 — Actual Orbit (mean distance from Sun)
1.0 — Orbit Predicted by Titius-Bode Law
All numbers are AU (astronomical units)

Jupiter 5.2 / 5.2
Saturn 9.54 / 10.00
Mercury 0.39 / 0.40
Venus 0.72 / 0.70
Uranus 19.2 / 19.6
Earth 1.0 / 1.0
Mars 1.52 / 1.60
Asteroid Belt 2.80 / 2.80
Neptune 30.1 / 38.8
Pluto 39.4 / 77.2

scientist he remained cautious, as revealed in a letter written to a colleague on January 24:

> I have announced the star as a comet. But the fact that the star is not accompanied by any nebulosity [cloudlike fuzziness, a common characteristic of comets] and that its movement is very slow and rather uniform has caused me many times to seriously consider that it might be something better than a comet. I would be very careful, however, about making this conjecture public.[13]

Eventually, Piazzi did tell other astronomers about the object he had seen. But after disappearing into the Sun's glare, it was temporarily lost and could not be confirmed. Fortunately, a German mathematician, Carl F. Gauss, calculated its orbit based on Piazzi's measurements. And using Gauss's data, on January 1, 1802, a year to the day after Piazzi had first seen the object, both Zach and another German astronomer, Wilhelm Olbers, found it again. The object, which everyone assumed was the missing planet, received the name Ceres, after an ancient Roman agricultural goddess.

"An Embarrassment of Riches"

It turned out that Ceres was not the missing planet, however. First, William Herschel estimated that it was much smaller than Mercury, the smallest known planet. Second, astronomers quickly started to find other small objects similar to Ceres. In March 1802 Olbers spotted one that became known as Pallas, named after an ancient Greek goddess. Then came Juno, named for an important Roman goddess, in September 1804 and Vesta, after another Roman goddess, in March 1807. Once astronomers worked out the orbits for these bodies, they saw that all of them were, like Ceres, located between Mars and Jupiter. Olbers, among others, began to suspect that all four objects, along with smaller ones yet unseen, were pieces of a major planet that had once existed in this region and had somehow broken up. "Could it be," he wrote in a letter to Herschel,

that Ceres and Pallas are just a pair of fragments, or portions of a once-greater planet which at one time occupied its proper place between Mars and Jupiter, and was in size more analogous to the other planets, and perhaps millions of years ago, either through the impact of a comet, or from an internal explosion, burst into pieces?[14]

Herschel agreed that this theory was plausible. He decided that since these objects were unlike other known objects in the solar system, they needed a name of their own; he called them asteroids, meaning "starlike objects." Naming them proved to be fitting

An artist's rendering of Ceres, the solar system's largest asteroid. Early nineteenth-century astronomers discovered Ceres by accident as they searched for an eighth planet.

because more and more of these asteroids came to light. In 1845 Karl Hencke discovered Astraea. And two years later he found Hebe. Also in 1847, J.R. Hind found Iris and Flora, and other searchers discovered Metis in 1848, Hygiea in 1849, Parthenope, Victoria, and Egeria in 1850. By 1852 the asteroid family had grown to twenty-three, and by 1868 astronomers had confirmed the existence of a hundred of these objects, all of them orbiting between Mars and Jupiter. Appropriately, the region lying between the two planets became known as the "asteroid belt."

Astronomers continued to use direct visual observation to find asteroids until 1891. In that year, German astronomer Max Wolf introduced a new, much more effective method for the search—photography. After mounting a camera on his telescope, Wolf made the first photographic discovery of an asteroid—named Brucia—in December 1891. (He knew it was an asteroid and not a star because he left the camera's shutter open for several hours; the stationary stars appeared as sharp dots on the photographic plate, whereas the moving asteroids left long trails of light on the plate.) Using this technique, Wolf was able to find four asteroids in a single night (September 7, 1896), considered an incredible achievement at the time. During his career, he discovered a total of 232 asteroids. This record was soon broken by his assistant, Karl Reinmuth, who found 284 asteroids.

Thanks to photography, literally thousands of asteroids were discovered in the early years of the twentieth century. So many new asteroids came to light, in fact, that astronomers lacked the time and resources to track and study them all properly. One of the most successful of the asteroid and comet hunters of that era, American amateur astronomer Joel H. Metcalf, put it this way:

The rapid and continuous multiplication of discoveries, since the invention of the photographic method for their detection, has introduced an embarrassment of riches which makes it difficult to decide what to do with them.[15]

Indeed, many astronomers became bored with finding asteroids and began to view them as useless cosmic garbage littering the heavens. In the 1930s, therefore, asteroid research came almost to a halt. It was not until about 1970, when the U.S. space program opened up fresh avenues for such research, that a new generation of astronomers showed renewed interest in asteroids. Among other things, the realization that both asteroids and comets might be remnants of the solar system's birth spasms spurred an avid effort to understand how these objects formed and what they are made of, an endeavor that is still ongoing.

Chapter 2

How Asteroids and Comets Formed

Up until about the middle of the twentieth century, astronomers still possessed an imperfect notion of how and where asteroids and comets originally formed. The theory that asteroids were the remnants of the explosion of an ancient planet still prevailed. Also, astronomers believed that the vast majority of asteroids inhabited the asteroid belt between Mars and Jupiter. As for comets, scientists assumed they were floating collections of sand and pebbles that formed and moved randomly through the solar system. When one of these objects happened to stray too close to a planet, the larger body's gravity pushed the comet into the inner solar system (the region inhabited by Mercury, Venus, Earth, and Mars). There the comet grew a tail and became visible to observers on Earth.

Eventually, however, astronomers were forced to revise their theories about the origins of asteroids and comets. They rejected the concept that the asteroids formed from the explosion of a planet that once lay between Mars and Jupiter. It became clear that the mass of all the bodies in the asteroid belt put together is no more than a small fraction of Earth's mass. Therefore, the asteroid belt does not contain enough material to make up a full-fledged planet. In addition, astronomers found asteroids in other parts of the solar system. Their efforts to explain how these bodies left the asteroid belt helped to create a better understanding of how asteroids formed.

Astronomers also gained a better understanding of comets. Some researchers pointed out that the floating sandbank model for these bodies was inadequate. It did not account for a comet's ability to form a tail repeatedly during multiple visits to the Sun's neighborhood. For a long time, the assumption had been that many of the sand grains making up a comet were coated with ice, which melted as the comet approached the Sun; the resulting vapors formed the tail. But the revisionists concluded that this amount of ice would be depleted in only a single pass at the sun. The comet could form many tails

As a comet nears the Sun, pockets of ice begin to change into gaseous form, contributing to the formation of a coma (cloud around the nucleus) and a tail.

over time only if it was a solid object made up largely of ice. This forced astronomers to reevaluate how comets formed, since icy bodies could only have formed in certain regions of the early solar system.

Formation of the Solar System

The revised vision of how asteroids and comets formed came to fit logically and neatly into the larger model scientists had developed to explain the formation of the entire solar system. This larger model is based on the solar nebula hypothesis (or nebular hypothesis), initially proposed in the eighteenth century by German philosopher Immanuel Kant and French mathematician Pierre-Simon Laplace. (The word nebula means a gaseous cloud.) According to the modern version of the theory, about 4.5 to 5 billion years ago the solar system developed out of a huge cloud of gases and dust floating through space. These materials were at first very thin and highly dispersed. But like all matter, they exerted a gravitational pull, which caused the particles of gas and dust to move slowly toward one another. More and more of the material fell toward the center, or core, of the nebula. And as this core grew increasingly compact, astronomer John Davies explains,

> it increased in mass and so generated a more powerful gravitational field. This in turn attracted in more material, increasing the mass of the core still further in a rapidly accelerating process. As material fell in towards the center, it was slowed down by friction [particles rubbing against one another] and gave up its . . . energy as heat, gently warming the central regions of the core. . . . As the cloud got more and more dense, a point was reached when . . . heat could no longer escape easily and the temperature at the center began to rise rapidly. After a while conditions reached the point at which nu-

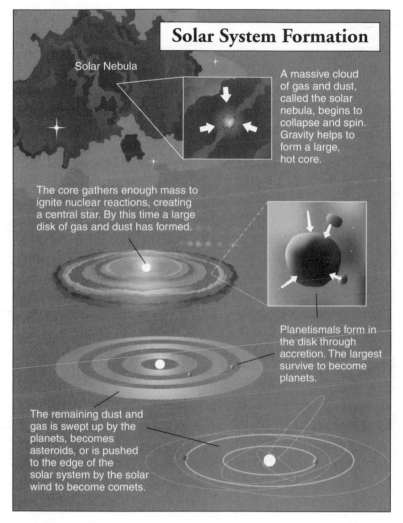

Solar System Formation

Solar Nebula

A massive cloud of gas and dust, called the solar nebula, begins to collapse and spin. Gravity helps to form a large, hot core.

The core gathers enough mass to ignite nuclear reactions, creating a central star. By this time a large disk of gas and dust has formed.

Planetismals form in the disk through accretion. The largest survive to become planets.

The remaining dust and gas is swept up by the planets, becomes asteroids, or is pushed to the edge of the solar system by the solar wind to become comets.

clear reactions could begin and . . . the star we call the sun was born.[16]

Most of the remaining material in the initial cloud formed a flattened disk that continued moving around the infant Sun. It was from this disk of material that the planets, moons, comets, and asteroids would form. The parts of the disk that were not too close to the hot star began to cool and solidify into small particles of rock and ice. At the same time, gravity caused the particles to accrete, or stick to one another, thereby creating larger particles. Over time, this process caused larger and larger clumps to form, some of which grew to be thousands of feet or even several miles in diameter. Astronomers call these large clumps planetesimals, essentially meaning "planetary building blocks." As time went on, many of the planetesimals continued to grow. According to Curtis Peebles:

> The planetesimals were ideal for sweeping up material. Like terrestrial [earthly] dustballs, the planetesimals had a loose, granular structure. The energy of any object hitting them would be absorbed, preventing it from rebounding. The object would be captured within the dustball. Once a few of the planetesimals had become larger than the others, they would begin to grow at an accelerated rate. Their gravitational attraction would begin to sweep up the surrounding dust, and the added mass would extend their reach. The process would affect objects of all sizes—dust grains would be trapped by tennis-ball-sized objects, which would then be captured by kilometer-sized planetesimals, which in turn would collide with objects made up of several planetesimals. The result would be large planetesimals that were loose aggregates [collections] of several smaller objects, all with differing compositions.[17]

The largest accumulations of planetesimals became the planets and their principal moons, while the smaller accumulations, along with many even smaller individual planetesimals, became the asteroids and comets.

Creation of the Asteroid Belt

The main factors that made asteroids distinct from comets in the early solar system were the types of materials that made up these bodies and their distances from the central Sun when they formed. The planetesimals in the inner solar system, close to the hot Sun, tended to be composed of harder, more heat-resistant materials. These included iron and other metals and various kinds of rock. Most of these metallic and stony planetesimals were swept up by and became part of the inner planets.

In contrast, the hard planetesimals lying near the outer edge of the inner solar system, just beyond Mars, were unable to accrete into a planet. This was because of their close proximity to Mars's outer neighbor, Jupiter. By far the largest planet in the solar system, Jupiter exerted a powerful gravitational attraction that constantly pulled and pushed on these objects, keeping them from accreting into one or perhaps two or three large planetary bodies. Instead, these planetesimals remained separate. In this way, the asteroid belt came into existence. This scenario explains why swarms of asteroids orbit where a planet should be, showing that the rough planetary pattern described in the Titius-Bode Law is essentially correct.

But not all of these millions of bodies were destined to float forever, quietly and unimpeded, in the dark expanse of the asteroid belt. This region proved to be a violent, turbulent place, as two major forces immediately went to work on the newly formed planetesimals. The first of these forces was the brute shock of repeated collisions. In fact, says planetary scientist Clark R. Chapman, collisions among asteroids are the dominant factor affecting the lives of asteroids as they hurtle through the vast reaches of the solar system. "Asteroids are miniscule [tiny]," he says,

> compared with the immensity of the [region] of space through which they travel. Yet there are enough of them moving sufficiently fast that major collisions are inevitable during the lifetime of the solar system for all but a lucky few asteroids. The typical collision velocity is about 5 km [3

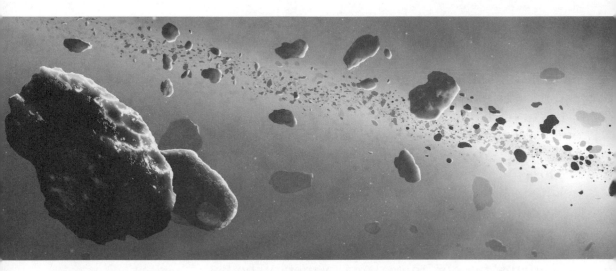

Millions of asteroids float in the asteroid belt after the solar system's formation. Jupiter's terrific gravity kept these objects from forming a planet.

miles] per second, involving a projectile that is most likely negligibly small compared to the target. Laboratory experiments and simulations suggest that for the largest impacts a typical asteroid might experience, the total energy is much more than sufficient to fracture and fragment an object having the material strength of solid rock. The only bodies that might be expected to survive such collisions more or less unscathed are (1) those with a cohesive strength exceeding that of iron, and (2) the very largest asteroids.[18]

The second major force working on the planetesimals in the asteroid belt was Jupiter's immense gravity. Its gravity not only kept the original planetesimals in the region from forming a planet but also grabbed hold of the larger ones and forcibly ejected them from the belt. In the words of scientist John A. Wood:

Jupiter eliminated them in the same way it removes material from the belt today. . . . The process might be likened to using a swing. Small pushes applied at exactly the right moment during each cycle of the swing, make it go higher and higher. [In a like manner, an asteroid whose orbit has been affected by Jupiter] may collide with another asteroid, dive into the inner solar system (often hitting a planet or the sun itself), or soar out to Jupiter's orbit or beyond. Ultimately, something almost certainly happens to remove it from the asteroid belt.[19]

The Kuiper Belt

The natural question is where did these asteroids go after Jupiter ejected them? As Wood points out, some ended up in the inner solar system, where they eventually collided with the inner planets or the Sun. Others left the solar system entirely, condemned to roam the black gulfs of interstellar space. Some of the ejected bodies, however, found new homes in the outer solar system, as Jupiter's gravity forced them into a belt of material lying beyond the orbits of the other three giant planets—Saturn, Uranus, and Neptune.

However, much of the material in this belt is not primarily metallic and stony in composition but, instead, largely icy. Indeed, the belt located beyond Neptune is a reservoir containing many of the planetesimals that formed in that cold region far from the Sun. As the early planetesimals were forming and growing, it was too hot in the inner solar system for ices to survive intact. Consequently, "most of the ices were evaporated and blown outwards," says Davies.

> Farther out . . . temperatures were low enough that ices could survive. So, as well as dust, the outer regions of the [original solar] disk contained considerable amounts of water ice and frozen gases such as methane, ammonia, and carbon dioxide. . . . [Beyond the giant planets], although there was sufficient material to reach the stage of forming small planetesimals, there was not enough time, or enough material, for them to combine into a

major planet. Instead, they formed a diffuse zone of icy objects in almost permanent exile at . . . the frozen boundary of the planetary region.[20]

The existence of this belt of icy, cometary material mixed with some asteroids and lying beyond Neptune was only recently confirmed. As early as the 1940s and early 1950s, two researchers—English astronomer Kenneth Edgeworth and Dutch-born American astronomer Gerard Kuiper—suggested that such a belt might exist. But it was not until 1992 that scientists began actually finding objects in the

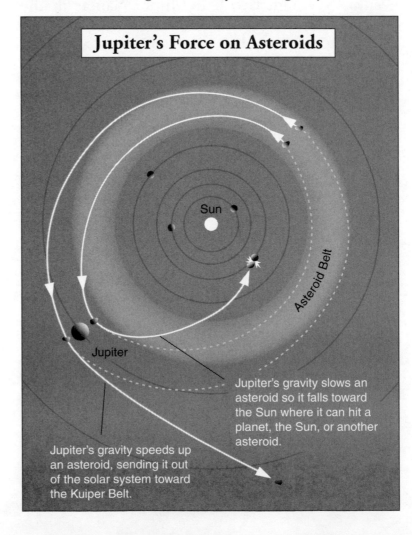

Jupiter's Force on Asteroids

Sun

Asteroid Belt

Jupiter

Jupiter's gravity slows an asteroid so it falls toward the Sun where it can hit a planet, the Sun, or another asteroid.

Jupiter's gravity speeds up an asteroid, sending it out of the solar system toward the Kuiper Belt.

Pluto: Planet or Giant Comet?

Since its discovery in 1930, Pluto has been classified as the ninth planet in the solar system and the farthest planet from the Sun. However, most scientists now recognize that Pluto began as a large Kuiper Belt object and, accordingly, some of them believe it should be demoted from its planetary status. Scientist Paul R. Weissman (in an article in *The New Solar System*, by J. Kelly Beatty et al.) explains this belief in the following excerpt.

Although it is generally labeled as a planet, many solar system astronomers think of Pluto as the largest icy planetesimal to grow in the region beyond Neptune. While Pluto has a satellite and a thin atmosphere, traditionally considered proof of planetary status, we now know of asteroids with satellites, and satellites with atmospheres. Moreover, Pluto is smaller than Titan, Ganymede, Callisto, and Triton—all satellites of the Jovian [gas giant] planets. Consequently, Pluto's classification as a planet has increasingly been questioned, especially given its dynamical similarities to other objects in the Kuiper Belt.

region. It became known as the Kuiper Belt in Kuiper's honor, and bodies in the belt are called Kuiper Belt objects, or KBOs for short.

The first KBO was discovered by astronomers David Jewitt and Jane Luu and designated 1992 QB_1. The object is approximately 190 miles in diameter and lies at a distance of 44 AU from the Sun. (AU is the abbreviation for "astronomical unit," the distance from Earth to the Sun, or about 93 million miles.) That is 14 AU beyond Neptune and about 4.5 AU beyond Pluto, the outermost planet. Only one-twenty-fifth the size of Mercury, Pluto is also the smallest planet in the solar system; many astronomers believe that it may be more accurate to call it a large KBO rather than a planet.

Other large KBOs have been discovered. In the spring of 2001, searchers found 2001 KX_{76}, also called Varuna, which is some 550 miles across. It is almost as big as Pluto's moon Charon (which is probably also a large KBO). An even bigger KBO about 800 miles across was found late in 2002.

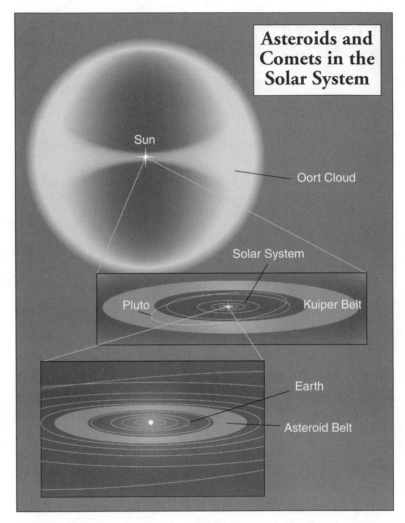

Dubbed 2002 LM_{60}, or Quaoar, it lies about 51 AU from the Sun (or about 21 AU beyond Neptune). To date, more than five hundred large KBOs have been discovered, and experts estimate that millions or even billions of others exist.

The Oort Cloud

Although many of the bodies in the Kuiper Belt are icy in composition and are therefore comets by definition, that region is not the only cometary reservoir in the solar system. Just as Jupiter's gravity expelled a number of asteroids from the asteroid belt, the gravities of Jupiter, Saturn, Uranus, and Neptune ejected most of the millions of icy planetesimals that formed in the neighborhood of these giant planets. Some of these comets fell into the inner solar system to be absorbed by the Sun and inner planets. And a few were hurled beyond the Sun's grasp into interstellar space.

Most of these objects, however, ended up in a vast shell of comets (and a few asteroids) lying beyond Pluto in the solar system's outermost frontier. Discovered in the 1940s by Dutch astronomer Jan Oort, it was named the Oort Cloud in his honor. "The Oort Cloud is the result of a long game of interplanetary pinball," says noted comet hunter David H. Levy.

> The youthful solar system was filled with comets— in Earth's primordial sky there must have been dozens of bright comets at a time. Some of the comets collided with the planets. Others made close passes by the planets, using their gravity to swing off into new orbits that would eventually land them near other planets. As the largest planet, Jupiter was the clear winner in this game. A comet swinging by Jupiter would get a gravitational hurl that would send the comet either out of the solar system forever, or off into the growing Oort Cloud. Within about 500 million years of the solar system's birth, the pinball game was all but over, its supply of cometary materials exhausted. . . . The process continues even today, but at a far more leisurely rate.[21]

Astronomers estimate that the Oort Cloud extends from about ten thousand to one hundred thousand AU or more from the sun and contains millions of small icy bodies. (The latest estimate is that about 2 percent of the objects in the region are actually metallic-stony asteroids tossed there by the giant planets.) From time to time, collisions cause some of these comets to leave the Oort Cloud and move into the inner solar system, where a few pass close enough to Earth to become visible to the naked eye.

The orbits of the comets in the Oort Cloud can also be disturbed by other stars that occasionally pass near our solar system. This is because these objects lie far enough out that the Sun's gravitational pull on them is barely enough to keep them from floating away. As Paul R. Weissman, of the Jet Propulsion Laboratory (in Pasadena, California), puts it:

> Oort showed that the orbits of the comets in the cloud were so weakly bound to the Sun that random passing stars could perturb them. Although stars rarely come very close to one another, on average about 10 to 12 stars must pass within 200,000 AU of the Sun every million years. Over the lifetime of the solar system, this is close enough to slowly stir the cometary orbits. . . . The perturbing influence of nearby stars also robs many comets of [their] momentum, causing them to "fall" toward the Sun and into the planetary region from all directions.[22]

Thus, the present structure of the solar system, including its reservoirs of asteroids and comets, reflects the manner in which it formed. The largest planetesimals became the planets and moons, while the smallest ones became the asteroids and comets. Most of the asteroids, made up of metal and rock, formed in the asteroid belt, and most of the comets, composed primarily of ices, ended up in the more distant Kuiper Belt and Oort Cloud. This more or less tidy situation was the result of the giant planets cleaning up and finding storage places for the asteroids and comets—the refuse created during the solar system's messy birth.

Chapter 3

Vital Statistics of Asteroids and Comets

"Imagine a package of rock and ice," David Levy challenges the reader,

a small world lost in the depths of space far beyond Pluto. No larger than a village, this world, which we call a comet, moves lazily around the Sun. . . . Suddenly, something—maybe a passing star—causes it to shift. Instead of moving around the Sun, the ball of rock and ice now moves in a new orbit that takes it closer to the solar system's central star.[23]

In this brief description of a comet floating in the distant Oort Cloud, Levy makes reference to the object's composition, its size, and its orbit, three of the four major vital statistics, so to speak, of comets. The other is the shape of such bodies.

Asteroids also possess vital statistics. Like comets, they can vary greatly in size, shape, and composition. And both kinds of cosmic bodies can move in a wide range of orbits, depending on such factors as where they formed, planetary and stellar gravitational attractions, and the force of random collisions. An added physical characteristic of asteroids is that some have satellites, or objects that orbit them, as many planets do. Clearly, the more scientists learn about asteroids and comets, the more varied and fascinating these objects seem.

Size and Shape

Perhaps the two most basic and visually obvious characteristics of asteroids are their size and shape. The largest known asteroid, as well as the first to be discovered—Ceres—is about 567 miles across, roughly the size of the state of Texas. This sounds very big. Indeed, all by itself Ceres contains about a quarter of the mass of all the known asteroids combined. On planetary scales, however, size can sometimes be deceiving. Approximately 4,000 bodies, each with Ceres' mass, would be needed to equal Earth's mass; and 318 Earth masses would be required to equal Jupiter's mass. So, the largest planet in the solar system is 318,000 times more massive than all of the asteroids put together.

Placing three well-known asteroids (Eros, Mathilde, and Gaspra) side by side provides a dramatic illustration of their irregular shapes.

Still, at least by human standards, Ceres and a number of other asteroids are very large bodies. In fact, twenty-six asteroids are more than 124 miles across, or bigger than the states of Massachusetts, Connecticut, and Rhode Island combined. The second-largest asteroid, Pallas, for example, is roughly 324

miles in diameter, somewhat larger than the state of Pennsylvania. Vesta is the third largest of the asteroids, with a diameter of 310 miles. Fourth comes Hygiea, which is 275 miles across; fifth Davida (208 miles); sixth Interamnia (207 miles); seventh Europa (187 miles); and eighth Juno (166 miles).

Astronomers have been observing the asteroid belt for so long that they believe they have found all of the large bodies inhabiting that region. In fact, nearly all of the asteroids in the belt that are bigger than sixty-two miles across have been discovered and inventoried. That does not rule out the possibility of finding more large asteroids in the future in either the Kuiper Belt or Oort Cloud. And of course, millions of smaller asteroids floating in the asteroid belt or elsewhere have not yet been discovered and cataloged.

Astronomers also point out that an asteroid's size and mass have a direct bearing on another vital statistic of these bodies—their shape. Like Earth and

Why Comets Have Odd Shapes

In this excerpt from their popular book on comets, Carl Sagan and Ann Druyan explain why small comets are not spherical.

Because the typical comet is so small, its gravitational pull is tiny. If you were standing on the surface of a cometary nucleus, you would weigh about as much as a lima bean does on Earth. You could readily leap tens of kilometers into the sky, and easily throw a snowball [into space]. . . . The Earth and the other planets tend to be almost perfect spheres because . . . gravity is a central force—it pulls everything equally toward the center of the world. . . . The mountains sticking up above the spherical surface of the Earth represent less of a deviation from a perfect sphere than does the layer of paint . . . on the surface of a typical globe that represents the Earth. . . . On a comet, on the other hand, the gravity is so small that odd, lumpy, potato-like figures would not be squeezed into a sphere. Such shapes are already known for the small moons of Mars, Jupiter, and Saturn. On a typical comet, you could build a tower reaching a million kilometers into space, and it would not be crushed by the comet's gravity [although the comet's rotation would throw it off into space].

the other planets, as well as their larger moons, the biggest asteroids are spherical. This likely includes Ceres, Pallas, and Vesta, each of which is more than three hundred miles in diameter, a size that may be an approximate dividing line between spherically and irregularly shaped cosmic bodies. Astronomer William K. Hartmann explains why larger asteroids are spherical:

> It is a question of strength of material. The larger the asteroid or planet, the greater the pressure at the center. If the central pressure exceeds the strength of the rocky material, the material will deform. . . . Higher internal temperatures also favor deformation toward a [spherical] shape.[24]

In contrast, smaller asteroids lack the mass to deform their materials into balls and are therefore irregular in shape. Single and especially multiple collisions experienced by these objects over the ages have also contributed to their uneven shapes. A typical example of such irregular asteroids is Eros, which NASA's NEAR-Shoemaker spacecraft explored in February 2001. Photos taken by onboard cameras revealed a lumpy, potato-shaped body some twenty-one miles long. Another asteroid studied up close by NASA, Gaspra, is also potato shaped and, like Eros, pitted with impact craters from numerous past collisions.

Asteroids come in many other shapes as well. Toutatis, for example, looks something like a dumbbell, with two distinct sections (2.5 miles and 1.6 miles across, respectively) touching in the middle. It appears likely that the two lumps were once separate asteroids. At some point in the past, the pull of gravity drew them together gently enough to keep them from fracturing into pieces. And now, they travel through the solar system locked in a strange embrace. Astronomers refer to dumbbell-shaped asteroids like Toutatis as compound asteroids.

Asteroidal Compositions

Asteroids vary not only in size and shape but also in composition. Scientists recognize a number of different types of asteroidal materials and usually classify asteroids by these types. The three primary categories are the C-types, S-types, and M-types. About three-quarters of all asteroids, including Ceres, Interamnia, Hygiea, and Davida, are C-types, which are characterized by a mixture of relatively lightweight carbon-rich minerals. Because these minerals are usually black or nearly so, C-type asteroids are very dark, so dark that they absorb most of the light that hits them. In fact, astronomers estimate that they reflect only about 5 percent of the sunlight that strikes their surfaces. For this reason, C-type asteroids are harder to see in telescopes than other kinds

Asteroid Types

	C-type (carbonaceous)	S-type (silicaceous)	M-type (metallic)
Composition	Relatively lightweight, carbon-rich minerals	Iron with iron- and magnesium-silicates	Mostly iron and nickel
Appearance	Very dark	Relatively bright	Relatively bright
Frequency	More than 75% of known asteroids	About 17% of known asteroids	Most of the rest of known asteroids
Location	Outer regions of main asteroid belt	Inner asteroid belt	Middle region of asteroid belt
Examples	Ceres, Interamnia, Hygiea, Davida	Eros, Gaspra, Juno	Eudora, Oceana, Psyche

of asteroids; Ceres is an exception because its unusually large size makes it fairly easy to spot.

On the other hand, S-type and M-type asteroids are easier to see because their materials reflect more light. S-type asteroids are made up of a combination of various kinds of metals and silicates (hard minerals composed of a mixture of silicon and oxygen compounds). Juno is a prominent example of an S-type asteroid. The M-types, which are apparently far less common than the other two types, are composed almost entirely of metals, particularly iron and nickel. The biggest known M-type asteroid is Psyche, with a diameter of roughly 163 miles, making it the single largest lump of metal in the solar system.

In general, these differences in the compositions of asteroids were the result of the positions these objects occupied in the emerging solar system. According to Curtis Peebles:

> The distribution of asteroid types matched that expected from several models of how the solar system condensed out of the original cloud of dust and gas. The silicate- and metal-rich types formed closer to the Sun, while those asteroid types composed primarily of lighter elements, such as carbon, condensed farther out. The same pattern is seen in the planets. Mercury, Venus, Earth, and Mars are all rich in silicates and metals, while the outer planets (Jupiter, Saturn, Uranus, and Neptune) are primarily hydrogen and carbon, with only limited percentages of silicates and metals. The asteroid belt is a dividing area between the realms of the two types of planets, and its composition reflects that change.[25]

Atypical Orbits and Asteroidal Moons

Other ways that astronomers classify asteroids are by how they orbit the Sun and the position they occupy in the solar system. Those lying in the asteroid belt between Mars and Jupiter are called "main belt" asteroids. The vast majority of asteroids, including Ceres, Pallas, Vesta, and most of the other large asteroids, are main belt bodies.

A number of much smaller clusters of asteroids are located outside the asteroid belt, two in the vicinity of the giant planet Jupiter. One of these clusters is pushed by Jupiter's gravity, so it always stays a little bit ahead of the planet as both travel around the Sun. The other cluster is pulled by Jupiter, so it moves along at a short distance behind the planet. Scientists call the asteroids that lie in these clusters the Trojans and have named the larger ones after heroes of the Trojan War, a famous conflict in Greek mythology. Among the Trojan asteroids are Agamemnon, Patroclus, Diomedes, Achilles, and Odysseus. The largest of all is Hektor, which is 186 miles long and 93 miles wide and probably a compound asteroid.

Also located outside the asteroid belt are several clusters collectively called the near-Earth asteroids, or NEAs. Of the three main clusters of NEAs, one, the Amors, features bodies that cross over Mars's orbit and come close to, but do not cross, Earth's orbit. As many as two thousand Amors larger than 0.6 miles in diameter may exist. Asteroids in the second major cluster of NEAs, the Apollos, actually cross over Earth's orbit. Astronomers estimate that up to one thousand Apollos larger than 0.6 miles across exist. The third major cluster, the Atens, has asteroids that orbit primarily inside Earth's orbit, so they are almost always closer to the Sun than Earth is. About a dozen or so Atens larger than 0.6 miles across are likely to exist.

The forces that cause the Trojans, Amors, Apollos, and Atens to find homes outside the asteroid belt are the same ones that eject asteroids and comets into the Kuiper Belt or Oort Cloud and out of the solar

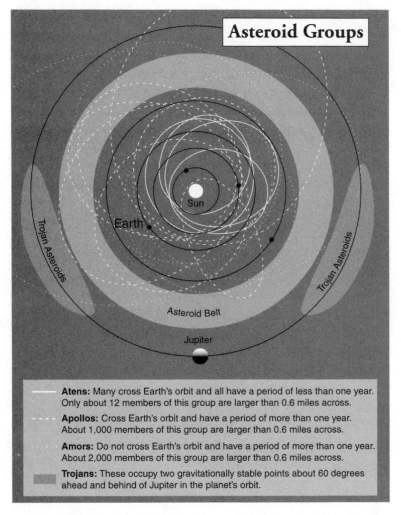

Asteroid Groups

Trojan Asteroids

Earth

Sun

Trojan Asteroids

Asteroid Belt

Jupiter

Trojan Asteroids

———— **Atens:** Many cross Earth's orbit and all have a period of less than one year. Only about 12 members of this group are larger than 0.6 miles across.

- - - - **Apollos:** Cross Earth's orbit and have a period of more than one year. About 1,000 members of this group are larger than 0.6 miles across.

········ **Amors:** Do not cross Earth's orbit and have a period of more than one year. About 2,000 members of this group are larger than 0.6 miles across.

▓▓▓▓ **Trojans:** These occupy two gravitationally stable points about 60 degrees ahead and behind of Jupiter in the planet's orbit.

system. Namely, the gravities of Jupiter, Mars, Earth, and the other planets capture these asteroids and fling them into unusual new orbits. Sometimes, however, the capture occurs but the fling does not. Astronomers believe that Deimos and Phobos, the two tiny moons of Mars, for example, are captured asteroids. Similarly, many of the satellites of Jupiter, Saturn, and Uranus are probably asteroids that strayed too close to and went into orbit around these giant planets.

In a similar manner, some asteroids manage to capture other asteroids. Indeed, astronomers have recently confirmed that some asteroids have satellites of their own. In 1993 NASA's Galileo probe flew near the asteroid Ida and discovered a tiny asteroidal moon, which the mission scientists named Dactyl. Dactyl is slightly less than a mile across, compared to Ida's thirty-five-mile diameter. Later, scientists found a moon eight miles across orbiting the asteroid Eugenia, which itself is 133 miles in diameter. Eugenia's satellite moves around the parent body once every five days. At first, astronomers assumed that these examples were rare exceptions. However, as Clark Chapman says, "Recent computer simulations of asteroid collisions now suggest that small [asteroidal] satellites might be fairly common."[26]

Dirty Snowballs

Like asteroids, comets come in many sizes and shapes, as do comets' nuclei, or solid heads. Most cometary shapes are irregular, as are most asteroids; however, if large icy objects like Varuna, Quaoar, and Pluto's moon Charon are giant comets, they may well be spherical. It is difficult to know for sure without close-up visual confirmation. (Unfortunately, these bodies appear as mere points of light even in the largest telescopes. This is because ice is lighter than the metal and rock that compose asteroids.) It is unclear how big bodies containing varying ratios of ice and rock must be to deform their materials into balls.

Comets are made up mostly of ice, although some have more ice or stony materials than others. The realization that comets are primarily icy bodies came in 1950. In that year, noted Harvard University astronomer Fred Whipple proposed what has come to be called the "dirty iceberg" (or "dirty snowball") model. The word dirty cannot be overstated, since the ices making up the bulk of a typical comet are not the clear, clean, reflective kind familiar on Earth. Instead, says NASA scientist Tom Duxbury, "They are the kind of snowball that the nasty kid down the street would make; full of sand and rocks and other stuff."[27]

Astronomer Fred Whipple demonstrates his "dirty snowball" model for comets with a five-hundred-pound snowball covered with dirt.

Astronomers believe that water ice is the most abundant of a comet's ices. Some of the frozen water exists in clathrates, mixtures of carbon dioxide, sulfur dioxide, and water ice, or in hydrates, mixtures in which water molecules are trapped within crystals of other substances. Frozen versions of the elements ammonia and methane are also present in considerable quantities in comets. In addition, the water, ammonia, and methane ices are riddled with molecules of poisonous substances such as hydrogen cyanide, carbon monoxide, and formaldehyde.

The fact that comets contain large amounts of water reveals a possible crucial relationship between them and Earth. Our planet has abundant water. Yet it formed in the inner solar system, where water and other volatiles (light substances that easily vaporize) did not form readily. Some water was trapped underground and later seeped to the surface. But much of it must have come from somewhere else, and comets are the most likely source. Comets that crashed into the young Earth may have brought other vital elements as well. "I think it is quite likely that most, maybe all, the carbon and nitrogen on Earth came from comets,"[28] says University of Hawaii astronomer Tobias Owen.

Forming a Tail

The ice and other volatiles that are the major constituents of comets also make it possible for these bodies to grow tails, their most notable physical property. A cometary tail forms by a process scientists

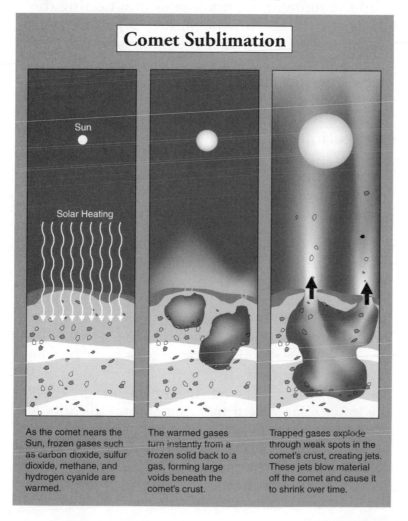

Comet Sublimation

Sun

Solar Heating

As the comet nears the Sun, frozen gases such as carbon dioxide, sulfur dioxide, methane, and hydrogen cyanide are warmed.

The warmed gases turn instantly from a frozen solid back to a gas, forming large voids beneath the comet's crust.

Trapped gases explode through weak spots in the comet's crust, creating jets. These jets blow material off the comet and cause it to shrink over time.

call sublimation, in which a solid turns directly into a gas, skipping the liquid stage. The most familiar example on Earth is "dry ice" (solid carbon dioxide), often used as a coolant. Unlike water ice, which changes into a liquid and then into a gas, dry ice sublimes into a white gas at temperatures exceeding –110 degrees Fahrenheit. In a like manner, many of the ices in the outer layers of comets sublime when these objects enter the inner solar system and sunlight begins to warm them. According to planetary scientist John C. Brandt:

> As a comet approaches the inner solar system, all the sunlight it absorbs goes into heating the nucleus. Closer in, the surface layers become warm enough to trigger the sublimation of ices. . . . As the ices vaporize, a dusty crust forms that insulates the deeper layers and regulates [the speed of] the sublimation process (now occurring a few centimeters below the surface). Irregularities in the materials cause sublimation to occur faster in some areas, a situation that can produce jets [the tail and the cloud around the nucleus] and ultimately the irregular shape and surface features of the nucleus.[29]

Eventually, this repeated loss of material caused by sublimation can result in a comet wasting away, the fate of most short-period comets. Short-period comets are those that originated in the Oort Cloud or Kuiper Belt, moved into the inner solar system, and were diverted by gravity during close passes to planets. In their new orbits, these comets make regular periodic swings through the planetary region. (In contrast, long-period comets are those that come from the Oort Cloud, enter the inner solar system to swing around the Sun, and then return to the Oort Cloud, often never entering the planetary region again.) A short-period comet's constant loss of material also makes it visually fainter than the average long-period comet. John Davies describes the cometary wasting process this way:

Pieces of Comet Shoemaker-Levy 9, which had earlier broken up after passing too close to Jupiter, slam into the giant planet in 1994.

Short-period comets approach the Sun very frequently and on each trip more and more of the volatile ices . . . are removed. So even when heated by the Sun . . . short-period comets are pale shadows of their fresh, bright cousins [the long-period comets] making their rare appearances in the inner solar system. The faintness of the short-period comets indicates that they are gradually running out of volatile material and that they cannot survive for long in their present orbits. The short-period comets are fated to fade away completely, and to do so quite quickly in astronomical terms. By estimating how much material is removed on every trip around the Sun, astronomers have shown that short-period comets cannot survive in their present locations for even a small fraction of the age of the solar system.[30]

Astronomers say that the fact that many short-period comets exist at any given time shows that their numbers are being replenished on a regular basis by new specimens floating in from the Oort Cloud.

Wasting away is not the only way a comet can lose its physical integrity. Some comets break up into two, three, or more pieces even before they run out of volatile materials. "Although we don't know for sure what makes them break up," states Zdenek Sekanina of NASA's Jet Propulsion Laboratory, "I believe one of the causes . . . is rotational breakup." Comets rotate fairly rapidly, he points out, and "if the spin is greater than the critical value [strength of gravity] that keeps the body together, they break up."[31] Moving too close to a planet can also make a comet break up. For example, in July 1992 Comet Shoemaker-Levy 9 passed within only twelve thousand miles of the cloud tops of Jupiter, the gravity of which tore the smaller body into twenty-one fragments.

Decline into Oblivion

For those comets that do not break up, their ultimate fates arise from a number of possibilities. As Brandt explains:

> Some are tossed out of the solar system altogether after passing near a massive planet. Others crash *into* a planet or satellite, or pass so close to the sun that they vanish in a cloud of dust. Those that do not go violently suffer a slow decline into oblivion. . . . If the comet initially had a rocky core, the end result becomes a member of an extinct-comet class of asteroids. In fact, [scientists] estimate that roughly one-third to one-half of all asteroids that cross or approach Earth's orbit are extinct comets.[32]

In this way, comets and asteroids are fundamentally linked, reminding earthly observers that both kinds of bodies formed in a like manner during the early years of the solar system's history.

Chapter 4

Voyages to the Comets and Asteroids

Until the 1980s, most theories about the composition and other physical characteristics of asteroids and comets could not be verified because no one had ever seen one of these bodies up close. Astronomers who studied them had to rely on images taken by ground-based telescopes. Even the largest telescopes revealed no distinct visual details, mainly because both asteroids (with the exception of Ceres) and comets are relatively tiny objects. And of course, they are also very far away. An astronomer on Earth trying to make out details on a one-mile-wide asteroid in the asteroid belt faces the same challenge as a person in New York trying to read words painted on a basketball in California.

Clearly, scientists realized, the only way they could solve the long-standing mysteries surrounding comets and asteroids would be to send spacecraft to study these objects up close. The first Earth probes to reach these objects were launched in the 1980s. And by 2003, more than a dozen spacecraft had flown by, orbited, or landed on one or more asteroids or comets. The information gathered during such exploratory missions has greatly expanded scientific knowledge of these important cosmic bodies. Many questions remain. But scientists are confident they will be answered by a number of other probes, some of which have already been launched.

The Pioneers

Today's asteroidal and cometary probes are all complex, sophisticated devices packed with state-of-the-art sensors, cameras, computers, and other instruments. In comparison, the first spacecraft to gather data about asteroids were much simpler and more technologically primitive. These craft, dubbed Pioneer 10 and Pioneer 11, were not designed to photograph or analyze any asteroids. Instead, they were intended primarily to explore the region around Jupiter. A secondary

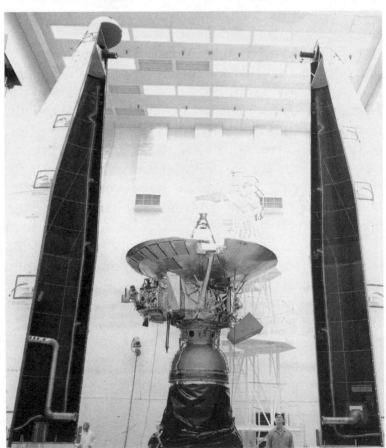

Pioneer 11 rests between the two halves of the nose cone of the rocket that will blast it into space.

goal of their missions was to assess the potential dangers that spacecraft would encounter while passing through the asteroid belt. At the time, many scientists theorized that billions of years of asteroidal collisions in this region had produced a dense clutter of rocks, pebbles, and dust; and they worried that Earth probes and ships might be damaged or even destroyed by this debris.

Pioneer 10 was launched in March 1972, and by July of that year it reached the asteroid belt. It carried two instruments designed to measure and record impacts of dust and tiny meteors (pieces of disintegrated asteroids and comets) both before and after entering the belt. The first of these instruments, Curtis Peebles explains,

> consisted of thirteen panels with 234 pressurized cells [each containing a gas]. . . . When a cell was hit by a meteor, the skin would be penetrated and the gas would leak out. Pioneer 10 had thin-walled cells; Pioneer 11's cells had a thicker skin, which allowed detection of only larger particles. The second experiment used a meteor-asteroid detector, a package of four telescopes that would detect the light reflected from a particle. . . . When any three of the telescopes saw an object, the experiment logged an event [i.e., an impact]. The object's relative size, distance, trajectory [direction of movement], and velocity could be calculated.[33]

During the journey to the asteroid belt, as Pioneer 10 moved through ordinary space, the instruments counted roughly forty small impacts. In comparison, forty-two impacts occurred while the craft was inside the belt. Pioneer 11, which launched in April 1973, recorded only seven small impacts inside the belt. These simple but effective experiments showed that the asteroid belt is not densely packed with debris and therefore is not unduly dangerous to human spacecraft.

Galileo snapped this photo of the asteroid Ida. The tiny object at right is Ida's satellite Dactyl, which is slightly less than a mile across.

The Galileo Mission

Though the Pioneer probes answered one important question about asteroids, many other questions remained. The next logical step was to fly by a large asteroid, photograph it, and send the pictures, via electronic signals, back to Earth. The first spacecraft to accomplish this feat was named Galileo. Launched by NASA from the orbiting space shuttle *Atlantis* in October 1989, the craft flew near two asteroids—Gaspra and Ida.

The Gaspra flyby took place in October 1991. Onboard cameras revealed an irregularly shaped object measuring roughly twelve by seven miles and pitted by close to forty large impact craters. These craters, along with several plainly visible fracture lines, suggest that Gaspra survived a major collision with another asteroid. Mission scientists estimated that the collision occurred between 300 and 500 million years ago. Other onboard instruments confirmed that the asteroid is S-type, composed of metal-rich rock.

Galileo's rendezvous with Ida took place in August 1993. Onboard cameras snapped about 150 photos in just under six hours, showing an uneven-shaped object about thirty-five miles long. The biggest surprise of the flyby, of course, was the discovery of Ida's moon, Dactyl. (Scientists initially called it "Baby Ida," but soon gave it the official title of Dactyl, after the Dactyls, magical beings who lived on Mount Ida in Greek mythology.)

At first, the existence of this asteroidal moon puzzled NASA scientists. They were fairly sure that Ida and Dactyl are fragments of a larger ancient asteroid that broke up in a collision event. If so, Peebles asks, "How could one body have ended up in orbit around another following such an event?" The scientists speculated, he says,

> that when the original body shattered, some of the fragments traveled along identical paths, flying side by side. As time passed, their gravitational attraction caused one to go into orbit around the other. Computer modeling indicated that if a 110-kilometer [68-mile] body shattered, there was a 50 percent chance that at least one of the larger fragments would attract a moon.[34]

Even as Galileo was investigating Ida and Dactyl, NASA was readying Clementine, a probe designed to fly close to another large asteroid. Clementine launched in January 1994 and headed for its intended target—an NEA named Geographos. Unfortunately, the spacecraft malfunctioned and the mission could not be completed.

Touchdown on an Asteroid

Many scientists felt that to some degree the spectacular success of the next asteroidal mission made up for Clementine's failure. In February 1996 NASA launched NEAR (which stands for Near Earth Asteroid Rendezvous) to study the asteroids Eros and

Mathilde. NEAR reached Mathilde, a main belt asteroid, on June 27, 1997. The flyby lasted only twenty-
five minutes but went according to plan and pro-
vided scientists with a bonanza of data. Onboard
cameras showed that the object is potato shaped and
measures about thirty-six by twenty-nine miles.

More importantly, it was discovered that Mathilde
has an eleven-mile-wide impact crater, a hole bigger
than Mount Everest and fully one-third the size of
the asteroid itself. When the great comet hunter
Eugene Shoemaker saw the first photo of Mathilde,
he quipped that "it is more crater than asteroid."[35]
Shoemaker and other scientists considered it incredible that the object had managed to survive such a
huge impact event.

Leaving Mathilde, NEAR headed for Eros, an NEA,
reaching it in December 1998. By this time, the craft
had been renamed NEAR-Shoemaker, in honor of
Shoemaker, who had tragically died in a car accident
in July 1997. The flyby showed that Eros measures
roughly twenty-one by eight miles. Also, like Mathilde,
it has an unusually large impact crater. The fact that
both asteroids visited by a single probe have such big
craters suggested to scientists that the materials making up these objects must not be very dense. Denser,
harder materials would have cracked and fragmented more easily, whereas less-dense materials
would better absorb large shocks.

NEAR-Shoemaker returned in February 2000 and
this time went into orbit around Eros. The mission
achieved another important milestone when, on
February 12, 2001, the intrepid spacecraft became
the first ever to land on an asteroid. Carefully guided
by scientists on Earth, the probe gently descended
toward the surface at about 3.5 miles per hour.
Touchdown occurred at 3:02 P.M. Eastern Standard
Time. "This was maybe the softest landing of all
time,"[36] mission director Robert Farquhar observed.
The final photos snapped by onboard cameras before

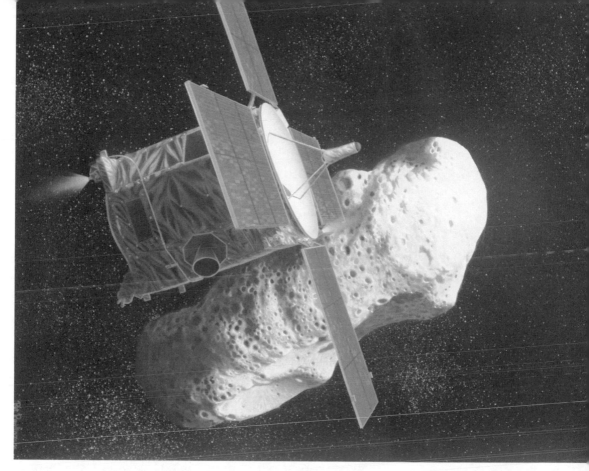

touchdown revealed surface details less than an inch across. Scientists are still examining and discussing these and NEAR-Shoemaker's other photos. They hope the pictures will help explain how rocks, pebbles, and other asteroidal surface materials crumble and shift position over time.

An artist's conception of NEAR-Shoemaker making its historic rendezvous with Eros. About a year later, the craft landed on the asteroid.

Topography of Asteroids

Still another Earth probe, the Jet Propulsion Laboratory's Deep Space 1 (or DS 1 for short), made it to an asteroid. DS 1 launched in October 1998, and in July 1999 it performed a flyby of the asteroid Braille (named for Louis Braille, inventor of the raised dot system that allows seeing-impaired people to read). This asteroid proved to be a peanut-shaped body measuring about 1.3 by 0.6 miles. From their analysis of Braille's surface materials, mission scientists concluded that it is a fragment that blasted off the larger asteroid Vesta in an ancient collision event.

These close-up studies of Braille, Mathilde, Eros, Gaspra, and Ida have vastly increased scientific knowledge of asteroids. In addition, the many detailed photos taken of their surfaces during these missions will prove valuable to companies that plan to conduct mining operations on these bodies in the next few decades. Indeed, knowing the topography, or the landscape characteristics, as well as the swift rotation periods, of asteroids is vital to such operations. "NEAR-Shoemaker's images of Eros and radar observations of several other small NEAs reveal a veritable zoo of irregular shapes," writes planetary scientist Daniel D. Durda.

Large ejecta blocks [pieces of rock dislodged during collision events], undulating [wavy] plains between overlapping large craters, and ridges and facets that define the overall shape of the asteroid could make for a wildly varying terrain with locally very steep slopes. On worlds the size of small towns, the horizon never lies far away—the vista over the other side of the next hill might well fall away beneath you to encompass the whole other side of the asteroid. Astronauts will also have to deal with rapidly changing lighting conditions. The rotation periods of many small NEAs are only a couple of hours, much shorter than the astronauts' spacesuits should allow them to explore. Surface crews may well witness several sunrises and sunsets during their excursions as they investigate their tumbling mountain.[37]

Rendezvous Party at Halley

While the Galileo and Clementine asteroid missions were still in the planning stages, scientists in the United States and other countries were also busy sending spacecraft to rendezvous with comets. The first Earth probe to perform a flyby of a comet was NASA's International Comet Explorer, or ICE

Deep Space 1:
On Technology's Cutting Edge

Here, from an article in the April 2002 issue of *Astronomy*, senior editor Richard Talcott describes the remarkable craft that successfully rendezvoused with Comet Borrelly—NASA's Deep Space 1.

On October 24, 1998, NASA's New Millennium Program got off to a rousing start with the launch of Deep Space 1. NASA designed this program to test cutting-edge technology in space. . . . Designed and built in just three years at a cost of approximately $150 million, the refrigerator-sized spacecraft flight-tested a dozen new technologies. Perhaps the most intriguing was an ion engine, a futuristic system that used . . . atoms [of the gas xenon] instead of standard chemical propellants. The engine created the ions by bombarding xenon atoms with a beam of electrons. It then generated thrust by passing the ions through an electrical field . . . and shooting them out the back of the spacecraft. . . . Among the other technologies used [was] a solar-power system that used cylindrical lenses to concentrate sunlight onto an array of solar cells. . . . Near the end of its primary mission, Deep Space 1 flew past the asteroid Braille. It then embarked on an extended mission that culminated with the Comet Borrelly flyby. . . . Engineers turned off the ion engine on December 18, 2001, though the radio receiver will be left on in case future generations want to contact the spacecraft [which is still in space today].

A composite of several images of Comet Borrelly taken by Deep Space 1.

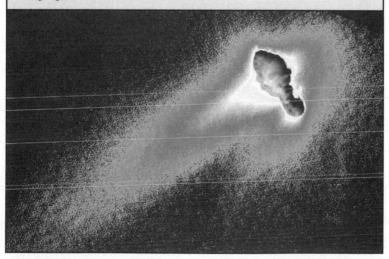

(originally named ISEE-3). Launched in August 1978, ICE reached Comet Giacobini-Zinner in September 1985. The craft first passed about 16,500 miles behind the comet, where it flew through and analyzed the gases and dust making up the tail. Then ICE briefly came within about 4,700 miles of the comet's nucleus before departing for its next and more high-profile cometary encounter.

That second rendezvous was with the most famous of all comets—Halley, which was then making its much publicized 1986 approach to the Sun and Earth. ICE was a latecomer to the Halley rendezvous party, however. The first Earth craft to reach the comet was the Soviet Union's Vega 1, on March 4, 1986, at a distance of about 92 million miles from Earth. Vega 1 got within about 5,300 miles of Halley's nucleus and snapped some photos, which were somewhat fuzzy and indistinct. A few days later, a sister craft, Vega 2, arrived, got a little closer to the comet, and produced better pictures. On March 8 and 11, respectively, two Japanese craft—Suisei and Sukigake—flew by Halley. Then, on March 13, the Soviet and Japanese probes were joined by Giotto, launched by the European Space Agency in July 1985. Giotto came within 373 miles of the comet and conducted its own close-up study, finally followed by ICE on March 28.

These spacecraft not only imaged Halley's nucleus but also analyzed the substances on its surface and in the halo of gas and dust surrounding the comet. For example, science writer William S. Weed points out,

> The Vega and Giotto probes found an abundance of water, gases, and primitive grains [pebbles] rich in elements that made up the solar nebula at the time the solar system was forming. The probes also detected complex hydrocarbons, the raw materials for life. Close-up photographs also revealed that

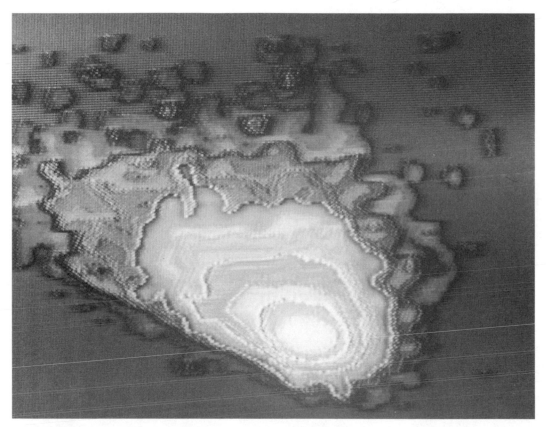

Halley was oddly shaped, not spherical as some had expected, and covered with . . . soot as if it had rolled down a dirty chimney. Astronomers think that [complex] molecules from comets can be deposited on Earth directly via impacts, or from the steady "precipitation" of particles from innumerable comet tails. The "dirty" part of Halley also includes silicate grains similar to what scientists find in meteorites.[38]

This is the first image of Comet Halley snapped by the European Space Agency's Giotto. Clouds of gas and dust surround the nucleus.

The spacecraft also studied the jets of gases that were shooting out of the comet and forming its tail. Scientists had anticipated that these volatiles would come mainly from the side facing the Sun, since it is presumably the warmth of sunlight that causes ices located near the comet's surface to sublime. And this is indeed what the Halley flybys confirmed.

"The bright jets visible in the images," reports John Brandt,

> originated from a limited number of locations on the comet's surface (perhaps one-tenth of the total area) and were confined to the sunward side. The jets appeared bright, presumably from sunlight reflecting off particles of dust dragged off the nucleus by the expanding, freshly sublimated gas.[39]

A New Generation of Explorers

Adding to the mountain of data gathered by the historic meeting of international spacecraft at Halley in 1986 was that generated by a mission to Comet Borrelly in September 2001. DS 1, which had rendezvoused with the asteroid Braille in 1998, passed within only 1,349 miles of Borrelly's nucleus. The

This artist's view shows NASA's Deep Impact spacecraft nearing a comet in 2005. If all goes well, the craft will become the first Earth probe to land on a comet.

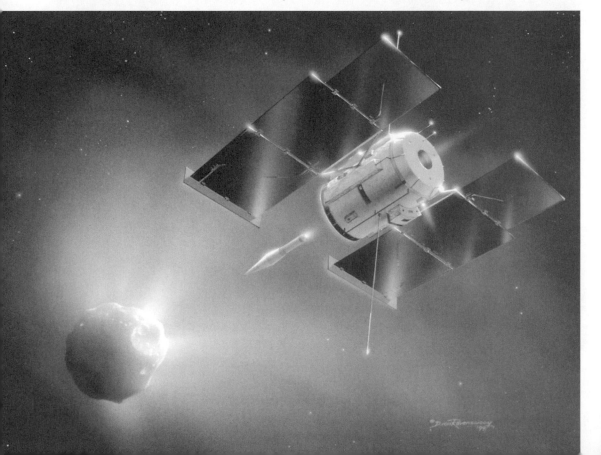

encounter was brief, as the probe rushed by the comet at 10.3 miles per second. But the photos snapped by DS 1's cameras were spectacular, the best ever taken of a cometary nucleus. In the words of Lawrence Soderblom, leader of the mission's imaging team, "These pictures have told us that comet nuclei are far more complex than we ever imagined. They have rugged terrain, smooth rolling plains, deep fractures, and very dark material."[40]

In fact, Borrelly, presumably like most or all comets, features a series of dark, rough-textured surface areas mixed with lighter, smoother ones. The jets forming the comet's tail are emitted from the lighter areas. So scientists think the jets regularly resurface these spots with fresh ices, while the darker areas are probably older, thicker material containing far fewer ices.

The mission to Comet Borrelly was the first of a new generation of cometary and asteroidal explorations slated by NASA for the early years of the new millennium. In 2004 a probe named Stardust will rendezvous with Comet Wild 2 and return to Earth with samples of comet dust. Samples of an asteroid will be gathered in the same manner by the Muses-C craft in 2005. That same year, another probe, Deep Impact, will be the first to land on a comet and use onboard instruments to analyze its ices. And the European Space Agency spacecraft Rosetta will land on and analyze the surface materials of the asteroid Wirtanen in 2011. Meanwhile, NASA's Contour probe will fly by three comets—Encke, Schwassman-Wachmann-3, and d'Arrest—by 2008. Astronomers and planetary scientists are clearly excited about what will surely prove to be a wealth of new knowledge about these surviving remnants of the solar system's violent birth.

Chapter 5

How Humans Will Mine Asteroids and Comets

The idea of mining the planets, Moon, asteroids, and comets for their valuable mineral resources is not new. Science fiction writers began weaving tales of space mines, worked by crusty, usually antisocial old prospectors, in the 1930s. Invariably, these difficult, dirty, lonely operations in the far frontiers of the solar system resembled the mines in a more familiar frontier situation—the nineteenth-century American West. There were "decadent boom towns with grossly inflated prices," University of Arizona scientist John S. Lewis points out in his recent book about space mining. These stories also featured "boisterous miners in town for a few days to pick up supplies and go on a bender," along with "slick gamblers, painted women, and a variety of dubious establishments."[41]

Not surprisingly, drunk miners, gamblers, and painted women were not part of the vision of the scientists who began discussing asteroid mining in the 1970s. The technological advances made during the U.S. space program had recently culminated in several successful manned Moon landings. And the experts became convinced that mining asteroids, and perhaps comets too, would actually be feasible in the near future.

Since that time, scientists working for both NASA and private companies have been doing detailed studies of space mining. The general consensus is that most of the technology needed to begin modest mining operations on an asteroid already exists. The main ingredient still missing is the commitment of a large amount of money by a government, corporation, or group of private investors. The experts all agree that it is only a matter of time before humans begin exploiting the tremendous wealth of resources waiting for them in the solar system.

An Extremely Profitable Business

The first questions that all potential investors ask, of course, are what is the nature of these abundant resources contained in asteroids and comets, and what are they worth? Scientists answer first that the asteroids are composed of iron, nickel, platinum, and other metals, as well as sulfur, aluminum oxide, carbon compounds, and other minerals. Many asteroids

Mining the solar system's riches was the subject of the 1981 movie Outland. *This shot from the film shows a mining colony on one of Jupiter's moons.*

also contain smaller amounts of volatiles, including hydrogen, oxygen, and water.

As for the value of these materials to people on Earth, Lewis cites the example of the smallest known M-type asteroid—Amun. It is about 1.2 miles across and has a mass of about 30 billion tons. To put this large tonnage in perspective, imagine that the raw materials from the mining operation are loaded into a fleet of space shuttles like those presently in NASA's fleet. The cargo bay of a typical shuttle holds about twenty-five tons, equivalent to 250 two-hundred-pound people. It would take four hundred shuttles (or four hundred trips by one shuttle), therefore, to haul ten thousand tons of asteroidal material; and it would take 1.2 billion shuttles (or 1.2 billion trips by one shuttle) to carry all of the materials mined from Amun.

Regarding the materials themselves, Amun's total tonnage breaks down into many different metals. The

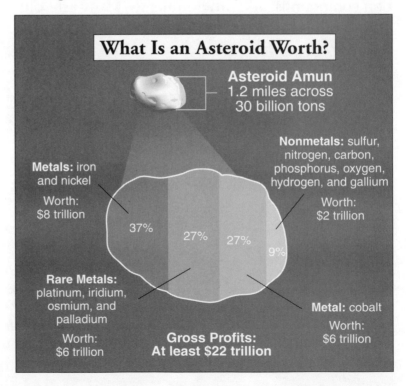

What Is an Asteroid Worth?

Asteroid Amun
1.2 miles across
30 billion tons

Nonmetals: sulfur, nitrogen, carbon, phosphorus, oxygen, hydrogen, and gallium

Worth:
$2 trillion

Metals: iron and nickel

Worth:
$8 trillion

37%   27%   27%   9%

Rare Metals: platinum, iridium, osmium, and palladium

Worth:
$6 trillion

Gross Profits:
At least $22 trillion

Metal: cobalt

Worth:
$6 trillion

most abundant of these are iron and nickel, which alone would have a market value of about $8 trillion. (Keep in mind that a trillion is a million times a million.) Supplies of another metal, cobalt, on Amun would be worth perhaps $6 trillion. Then there are rarer metals such as platinum, iridium, osmium, and palladium, which together would add another $6 trillion to the investors' profits. The nonmetals, including carbon, nitrogen, sulfur, phosphorus, oxygen, hydrogen, and gallium, would be worth at least $2 trillion. If humans mined all of Amun, therefore (which would take many years), the gross profits would come to at least $22 trillion. It is difficult to estimate the upfront costs of such a mining operation. But even if they were as high as $1 trillion, the net profits would still be $21 trillion. Clearly, asteroid mining will be an extremely profitable business.

Remember also that all of the valuable resources and profits cited are from a single small asteroid. What would all of the asteroids in the asteroid belt together be worth? Lewis speculates about the asteroidal iron alone:

> To raise the standard of living of the people of Earth to present-day North American, Japanese, or Western European levels, we need about 2 billion tons of iron and steel each year. With the asteroidal supplies of metal at hand, we could meet Earth's needs for the next four hundred million years. . . . Suppose that we were to extract all the iron in the belt and bring it back to Earth. Spreading this amount of iron uniformly over all the continents gives us a layer of iron . . . half a mile thick. . . . This is enough iron to cover all the continents with a steel frame building 8,000 stories (80,000 feet, or 15.2 miles) tall.[42]

When one factors in the other metals available in the asteroid belt alone, along with the many nonmetals, the total resources could sustain a human population a million times larger than the present one for several thousand years. And this does not take into account the trillions of asteroids and comets in the Kuiper Belt and Oort Cloud. (The comets contain far fewer metals, but do have many minerals, as well as an abundance of volatiles that could be used for food production and making fuels.)

Supplies for Earth and the New Frontier

The discussion of the monetary worth of asteroids and comets must not divert attention from the other major reason to pursue the dream of mining these objects. Namely, the metals, minerals, and volatiles acquired in such operations would help conserve supplies of these materials on Earth. At present, these supplies are marginally sufficient to sustain the planet's present population. But that population will inevitably grow and supplies of a number of metals and other commodities will begin to run out.

Also, processing metals and minerals (separating them from the rocky mixtures in which most are trapped) pollutes Earth's air, soil, and water. This problem will be eliminated entirely in space mining since all of the processing will take place far from Earth. At first glance, it would seem that such operations would simply shift the pollution problem from Earth to outer space. But this need not be the case. William Hartmann explains:

> Some writers have raised the specter of humanity despoiling the solar system, in the same manner that over-industrialization is beginning to despoil Earth's environment. But . . . with a careful balance of research and exploitation, we could learn from and process materials in space in a [clean] way that would [also] begin to take the pressure off Earth's ecosystem. A transition from Earth-based manufacturing to interplanetary manufacturing could eventually reduce pollution and ravaging of

Earth by an Earth-based society bent on ripping the last dwindling resources from the land.[43]

There is another dimension to human acquisition and consumption of cosmic resources, however. Nearly all the experts agree that by the time space mining becomes widespread, only a small percentage of the materials mined will end up on Earth. Instead, a major portion of these resources will be used to construct and sustain human colonies and cities floating in space. Space, they say, will become a vast new frontier that will attract many people born on Earth, helping to stabilize or at least slow the growth of the planet's population. (And of course, over time even more people will be born in space.)

It is fair to ask why the inhabitants of such colonies, as well as people still living on Earth, would choose to get metals, minerals, and other resources from asteroids and comets rather than from larger cosmic bodies. Why not mine the Moon first, for example, or perhaps the planet Mars? After all, the Moon and Mars are both far larger than all of the asteroids put

A City in the Sky

As planetary scientist John S. Lewis says in this excerpt from his fascinating book *Mining the Sky*, the asteroid belt contains enough iron to construct an enormous space city.

We have enough asteroidal iron [in the asteroid belt] to make a metal sphere . . . 550 miles in diameter. Hollowed out into rooms with iron walls, like a gigantic city, it would make a spherical space structure over . . . 1,200 miles in diameter. . . . With a nine-foot ceiling, we could provide each family with a floor area of 3,000 square feet for private residential use and still set aside 3,000 square feet of public space per family. This artificial world would contain enough room to accommodate more than ten quadrillion [a million times a billion] people. Very simply, that is a million times the ultimate population capacity of Earth.

together, and both are closer to Earth than most of the asteroids and comets (the NEAs being an obvious exception).

First, whether they live on Earth or in space cities, people will naturally want to obtain cosmic resources as easily and cheaply as possible. The fact is that mining the asteroids will be far easier and more economical than mining a large body like the Moon. The Moon's surface gravity is about one-sixth that of Earth, which is strong enough to require a good deal of fuel to land miners and their equipment on its surface. More importantly, getting the processed metals and minerals off the Moon's surface would take even larger amounts of fuel. An added problem is that most of the valuable metals and minerals on the Moon are spread out over thousands of square miles and bound up inside mixtures of rock and dirt, many lying deep underground; it would require a lot of exploration, as well as strenuous and expensive digging and processing, to free them.

Zero-Gravity Mining Techniques

In contrast, most asteroids and comets are small, manageable, and have extremely tiny gravities, all of which make them easier to mine. Mining ships will also not land on or take off from these bodies, which will save enormous amounts of fuel. A typical ship will stop beside an asteroid and the miners, wearing spacesuits, will transport over to the worksite by pushing off the side of the ship. (They may also use small jets attached to their suits.) This is possible because the ship, the miners, and the asteroid are all nearly weightless. For this reason, the miners will need to attach long tethers to their suits and tie the opposite ends of the tethers to spikes hammered into the asteroid. This will keep them from accidentally floating away into space while they are working.

In addition, the mined materials in such a situation are, like the miners, nearly weightless, and will

In this illustration of an asteroid mining operation, an astronaut is tethered to the surface. He uses a jet pack to maneuver.

not need to be lifted off the asteroid's surface. This will not only save fuel, but will greatly reduce other risks. According to the scientists at the Minor Planet Center (at the Smithsonian Astrophysical Observatory):

> Getting asteroidal materials is not a risky business, like launching materials up from Earth or the Moon. Transporting asteroidal materials is all "interorbital" [i.e., takes place in orbit]. [There will be] no risks of crashes, no huge rockets. The gravity of the asteroids is negligible. A person can jump off any but the largest asteroids with leg power alone.[44]

Another advantage of mining asteroids rather than the Moon is that the asteroidal metals and minerals are concentrated in a small, easily accessible space and are much purer in content. Almost all asteroids, Daniel Durda points out, "have a hundred times more metal not bound up in rocky minerals than do moon rocks."[45] On S-type and especially M-type asteroids, such materials will require very little processing. Indeed, a fair amount will be collectable even before the digging process begins. The surface of such bodies is rich in granules of metal, ranging from sand- to perhaps fist-sized pieces, all mixed with sootlike dirt. These granules "can easily be separated from the dirt," the Minor Planet Center experts say,

> using only magnets [in the form of magnetic rakes] and soft grinders. Some engineering designs have "centrifugal grinders," whereby the dirt is fed into a rotating tank and shattered against the wall a time or two. Out come little metal disks, which are separated using simple magnets.[46]

Once digging operations begin, larger deposits of metals and minerals will be separated with bigger grinding and chopping devices. Most likely, the miners will allow the loose rocks to float up and away from the asteroid's surface, where a large canopy, a sort of tarp made of nylon or some other tough material, will catch them. One group of experts describes the advantages of such a canopy:

> Companies will most probably use a canopy because the canopy would be quite profitable in terms of the amount of loose ore [rock mixture] it would collect. It would also prevent the area [around the worksite] from turning into a big dark cloud of debris which would pose problems for the operations. . . . A double-cone-shaped canopy is put around the asteroid. . . . The canopy is then rotated. A [small robotic device called a] dust kicker goes down to the asteroid and . . . kicks up the ore at low velocity. The ore strikes the canopy and is deflected so that it tends to rotate with the canopy, eventually sliding down the two [cone-shaped] funnels.[47]

The equipment for processing the metal- and mineral-rich ore will be located at the tips of the two cones. After all of the usable materials have been mined, the miners will tie off the ends of the canopy and tow it either to a floating city or into Earth's orbit. That way, the canopy doubles as both a collection apparatus and transport device.

Habitats for the Miners

During these mining operations, which could take months or years, depending on the size of the asteroid and the number of workers and machines, the miners will need somewhere to live. The quarters aboard the ship itself will likely be too cramped for such a long stay. So the miners will build a temporary habitat, which will use mostly on-site materials and thereby eliminate the need and cost of bringing them from Earth.

To some degree, the kinds of materials required to erect and sustain a human habitat for such miners will dictate the type of asteroid the mining operation will target. Although M-types have more metals than other kinds of asteroids, probably a majority of the asteroids mined will be S-types or C-types. These bodies have larger supplies of oxygen, hydrogen, water (in the form of ice), and other volatiles that are essential to the habitats. If necessary, additional volatiles can be obtained from comets; storehouses of cometary volatiles could be positioned at various points in space for asteroid miners to draw from.

As for how these lighter materials will be converted, first the miners will melt the ices to produce water for drinking, cooking, and bathing. They will also extract oxygen and hydrogen from the ices and combine them with various minerals to make beams, walls, pipes, and other parts for their habitat. The miners can also employ the oxygen and hydrogen to make fuel, both to power the ship on its return voyage and to sell to companies or individuals

In a scene from Outland, space miners are shown in a habitat built on-site. Large versions of such habitats will feature most of the comforts of home.

in space cities or on Earth. This means that relatively little, if any, fuel will have to be brought from Earth, making space mines and habitats almost completely self-sufficient.

Indeed, nothing would be wasted during the mining operation. "Even unprocessed soil," says Durda, "could be used for shielding" to protect miners and other astronauts "on longer missions from cosmic rays and solar flares [dangerous radiation from the Sun]."[48]

Setting Large-Scale Goals

These mining situations and techniques are not some flight of fancy that will take centuries to become reality. NASA, various groups of scientists, and some private companies have already begun drawing up plans for such space mining missions. They know that certain inherent difficulties and problems will have to be overcome, or at least planned for, to make this huge undertaking work. For example, even in the case of the NEAs, which will surely be the first targets for space miners, a typical round trip will be two to five years. This is a long time for a company of miners to be separated from family, friends, and society in general. Long periods of work in weightless conditions may also have a negative effect on the miners' health. Astronauts who have spent many months in weightless conditions in Earth's orbit have developed muscle weakness, loss of calcium and red blood cells, and other problems. And of course, such ventures will be extremely costly and require long-term financial and other commitments from governments, companies, and tens of thousands, if not millions, of individuals.

Assuming such commitments do materialize, however, the technical difficulties will be relatively minimal. Indeed, scientists emphasize that humans can reach and mine the asteroids and comets mostly using technology that exists or is presently in development. It is true that this technology will have to be applied on a much vaster scale than people have ever experienced. But it is doable nonetheless. "This isn't Star Wars," say the Minor Planet Center researchers. "The asteroids aren't against us. It's really pretty simple stuff." People have already demonstrated the ability to travel and live in space, and "the engineering factors that go into 'docking' with an asteroid are not difficult."[49]

The biggest difficulty will rest in the human decision to begin the mammoth enterprise of exploiting the riches of the solar system. Countries, peoples, and governments have accomplished such large-scale goals before, as the Europeans did when they settled and transformed North and South America or as the Americans did when they aimed for and reached the Moon in the 1960s. One thing is certain. These prior undertakings, though enormous in their own times, will be positively dwarfed by the adventure that awaits humanity in the asteroid belt and beyond.

Chapter 6

When Comets and Asteroids Strike Earth

Mining some of the near-Earth asteroids will exploit the considerable constructive potential of these cosmic bodies. However, many of the NEAs have a darker, more *de*structive potential as well. Namely, those NEAs that cross Earth's orbit can occasionally be attracted by the planet's gravity (or the Moon's gravity) and end up striking Earth.

The reality of this threat is demonstrated by the fact that small pieces of older, disintegrated comets and asteroids enter Earth's atmosphere all the time. Indeed, tens of thousands of these meteors do so each day. Most burn up in the upper atmosphere, where at night their rapid streaks across the sky are often erroneously called "shooting stars." Occasionally, larger meteors make it through the atmosphere intact and strike the ground (in which case they become known as meteorites). A number of such strikes have been witnessed and the objects recovered. One of the most celebrated cases occurred in November 1492 in Germany, where a crowd of people saw a falling object and later dug it up. It was a few feet across and weighed some three hundred pounds.

Such relatively small rocks falling from space usually cause little damage or injury. However, the danger increases considerably when these cosmic missiles are only marginally larger. An object the size of a large house could easily wipe out a good-sized city. And the impact of an asteroid or comet a little more than half a mile across would release about 1 million megatons of energy (several million times more than the energy released by the atomic bomb dropped on Hiroshima, Japan, in 1945). This would be enough to create a global catastrophe that would kill hundreds of millions of people and animals.

Meteors burn up in Earth's upper atmosphere. Thousands of small meteors enter the atmosphere each day.

Cosmic Impacts Only in the Past?

Unfortunately, many people assume that such large-scale disasters happened long ago, before humans appeared on Earth. This is partly because of widespread publicity in recent years about the enormous mass extinction that occurred 65 million years ago when a large comet or asteroid struck the planet. Among the victims were the dinosaurs. The natural human tendency is to believe that this event was a rare fluke, a thing of the past, and that Earth is now largely safe from such global disasters. However, the truth is that such events can happen at any time. According to astronomer Gerrit L. Verschuur:

It is nearly impossible to admit that our lives might be

This photo of the Moon shows an amazing density of impact craters. The large crater at top-center is called Daedalus.

wiped out through a whim of nature, a chance event, and that may be why it has been so difficult to allow that dramatic mass extinctions of the past happened suddenly. It is even more difficult to admit that another such catastrophe might be triggered by a random collision between the Earth and an object from space. This is the unpleasant likelihood suggested by the data. . . . We assume that mass extinctions happened long ago and that nothing similar will happen again. This scenario is false.[50]

Thus, it is not a question of *whether* a comet, an asteroid, or a piece of one of these bodies could impact Earth. It is merely a question of *when*. Indeed, studies of past impact events reveal that such disasters, far from being rare, have occurred on a regular basis throughout the planet's history. It happened when Earth was forming, for example; for millions of years, planetesimals of all sizes rained down on our infant planet. Comets and asteroids struck the Moon as well. The Moon has about three hundred thousand impact craters with diameters of 0.6 of a mile or more. These craters have survived intact because the Moon has no air and water to erode them. In contrast, Earth, which is larger and has a more powerful gravitational pull than the Moon, has suffered far more asteroidal and cometary impacts. Very few impact craters are visible on Earth, however. This is because the effects of rain, wind, tides, volcanoes, and so forth have eroded and erased most of them.

Among the few large impact craters still visible on Earth's surface, the youngest and best preserved is Barringer Crater (also called Meteor Crater), near Winslow, Arizona. The crater is about three-quarters of a mile wide and some six hundred feet deep. The event that caused it to form occurred roughly fifty thousand years ago. (Fortunately, no people were killed in the blast because early humans had not yet migrated to North America.) University of California

Scientist Eugene Shoemaker poses on the rim of Arizona's Barringer Crater, which formed from the impact of a metallic asteroid.

geochemist Alan E. Rubin provides this overview of the immense explosion:

> The crater was produced by the impact of a 50-meter [164-foot]-diameter metallic iron projectile that liberated an amount of energy equivalent to 20–60 megatons of TNT [several thousand times larger than the Hiroshima explosion]. The explosion excavated a depression 150 meters [492 feet] below the surrounding plains. . . . More than 100 million tons of rock were thrown from the crater. . . . At the instant of impact, a shock wave was produced that raced through both the target and the projectile. . . . A powerful air blast was caused by the shock wave, scouring the landscape with wind speeds exceeding 1,000 kilometers [620 miles] per hour. Trees and grasses were uprooted, and the Ice Age animals within a few kilometers of the crater were killed either by the air blast itself or by being pelted with branches, stones, and sand.[51]

The K-T Event

In human terms, this disaster seems big and frightening. But it pales in comparison to the explosion and loss of animal life in the impact event that occurred some 65 million years before. The comet or asteroid that collided with Earth at that time was about six miles across and traveling somewhere between twelve and forty-two miles per second. It struck the shallow ocean near the eastern coast of Mexico with the almost incomprehensible force of 100 million megatons (some 5 billion times more powerful than the Hiroshima explosion).

Within a second of the impact, an immense fireball formed. It created a powerful atmospheric shock wave that expanded outward in all directions. Every tree was leveled and every living thing was killed up to a distance of at least a thousand miles. Meanwhile, the impact carved out a crater about ten miles deep

This illustration of the K-T impact emphasizes that the dinosaurs were among the many victims of the catastrophe.

and more than a hundred miles in diameter and set off giant earthquakes that raised the ground in waves hundreds of feet high. Also, giant sea waves pounded the coastlines of the planet, crushing or drowning all animals in their path.

Later effects of the catastrophe were even worse. The explosion threw millions of tons of ash and dust into the atmosphere, blocking sunlight for many months. This made Earth's surface very dark and cold and destroyed most of the surface plants, causing most of the planet's food chain to collapse. Roughly 70 percent of all the animal and plant species on Earth, including all of the dinosaurs, died.

This global calamity, which scientists call the K-T event, was important not only for its effects on Earth and the animal kingdom in general but for the subsequent course of evolution, especially the rise of human beings as the dominant life-form on the planet. It is almost certain that the spread and ultimate success of large mammals, including humans, would not have occurred (or at least not in the same manner) if the dinosaurs had survived. If the dinosaurs "had not been wiped out," Verschuur points out,

> mammals would not have arisen to dominate the world in their stead. After the dinosaurs were ushered off the terrestrial [earthly] stage, the scene was set to allow mammals to diversify until, 65 million years later, one of their kind, *Homo sapiens*, rose to prominence. Our species recently evolved to become conscious and clever enough to invent agriculture, technology, and science, and we have used our newly developed mental skills to uncover the secrets of nature that carry the clues to our origins, and to our future. To put this another way, if the comet that triggered the K-T event had arrived twenty minutes earlier or later, it would have missed the planet and we would not be here now, talking, reading, or writing about any of this.[52]

This map shows the location of some of the major known impact craters on Earth. The one formed by the K-T event can be seen on Mexico's eastern coast.

City Destroyers

Disasters on the huge scale of the K-T event happen perhaps once every 50 to 100 million years.

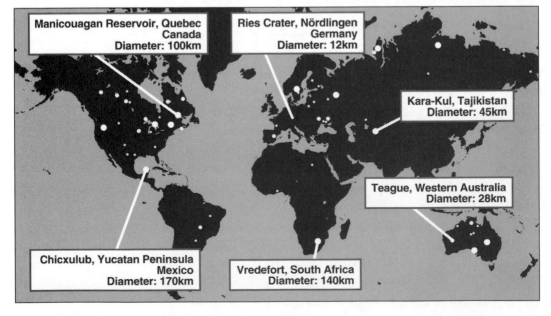

Manicouagan Reservoir, Quebec
Canada
Diameter: 100km

Ries Crater, Nördlingen
Germany
Diameter: 12km

Kara-Kul, Tajikistan
Diameter: 45km

Teague, Western Australia
Diameter: 28km

Chicxulub, Yucatan Peninsula
Mexico
Diameter: 170km

Vredefort, South Africa
Diameter: 140km

But smaller cometary and asteroidal impacts capable of destroying one or several cities occur much more frequently. In fact, one such disaster happened as recently as 1908 when an object about the same size as the one that created Barringer Crater exploded over Tunguska, a remote area of eastern Russia. Forests were completely flattened for a distance of almost twenty miles from ground zero. But few people lived in the region, so the loss of human life was very small. Still, even those who lived far from the impact site were startled and in some cases injured by the effects of the blast. One eyewitness who had been about sixty-six miles away from the impact later reported:

> Suddenly . . . the sky was split in two and above the forest the whole northern part of the sky appeared to be covered with fire. . . . I felt great heat, as if my shirt had caught fire. . . . There was a . . . mighty crash. . . . I was thrown onto the ground about [twenty feet] from the porch. . . . A hot wind, as from a cannon, blew past the huts from the north. . . . Many panes in the windows [were] blown out.[53]

Another reason that the death toll from the Tunguska impact was small was that the object struck land rather than sea. If the same object, or one larger, had struck the ocean, it would have generated huge sea waves, or tsunamis. The fireball of a large asteroid or comet striking the ocean would blast through the water and in only a few seconds carve out a crater many miles wide and thousands of feet deep in the seabed. John Lewis explains how tsunamis would be generated by such a strike:

> The water displaced from the explosion cavity is partly ejected in a broad, open cone at many times the speed of sound. The seabed is cracked by the blast wave, melted and scoured by the

one-hundred-thousand-degree fireball. Hundreds of cubic kilometers of water are vaporized, blasting an immense column of steam back out to space. . . . When the surface of the fireball coasts to a stop in the water, the ocean surface collapses back into the cavity . . . from all sides, converging on the center of the crater. As the wave crest approaches the center of the crater, fast-moving waves converging from all directions pile into each other, rushing headlong into a monstrous surge that shoots up a towering pillar of water higher than the highest mountains on Earth. The sea sloshes back and forth in the blast region, pumping the surrounding ocean and generating circular wave fronts which, like the ripples from a pebble tossed into a puddle, spread out in all directions.[54]

As such waves approach land, they can grow to towering heights. The waves generated from a one-thousand-megaton strike (about twenty times larger than the Tunguska explosion), for instance, would be well over five hundred feet high, as tall as a fifty-story building. These could easily destroy one or more cities.

Warnings of Cosmic Perils

The destruction of a city, or perhaps dozens of cities, by the effects of a cosmic impact would naturally be appalling. But at least most of the human race would survive. However, if a comet or asteroid the size of the one that caused the K-T event, or one even larger, were to strike, humanity might not be so fortunate. A warning of the possible perils that await Earth in the depths of space came in 1994 when twenty-one pieces of the recently fragmented Comet Shoemaker-Levy 9 plowed into Jupiter. At just over a mile across, each piece blasted a hole the size of Earth in Jupiter's upper atmosphere. If these twenty-one cometary fragments had struck Earth instead, all life on our planet would have been annihilated.

It is impossible to say for sure how likely it is that such an object will hit Earth in the near future. However, if recent strikes and near misses are any indication, events that could kill millions of people could potentially occur at least once, and perhaps as many as three times, per century. In 1890, people in Capetown, South Africa, witnessed a comet as it passed rapidly by Earth at a distance of fifty thousand miles, only one-fifth the distance to the Moon. The Tunguska event occurred in 1908. And in 1992, a comet missed our planet by only twelve thousand miles. Some experts estimate that the impact of this object would have generated an explosion of fifteen thousand megatons. If it had struck land, it would have annihilated most life in an area the size of the state of Texas; if it had plunged into the sea, it would have generated tsunamis thousands of feet high, killing even larger numbers of people.

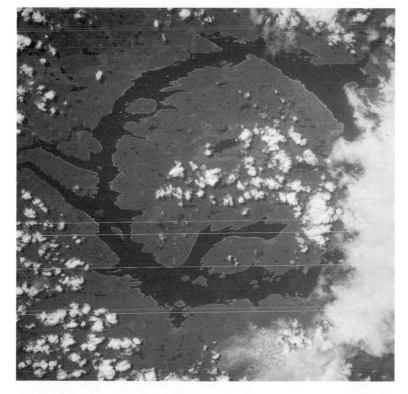

This photo taken from an American space shuttle shows Canada's Manicouagan Reservoir, an impact crater that formed about 212 million years ago.

Looking into the future, astronomers have calculated that an even bigger object—Asteroid 1950 DA— is likely to strike Earth on March 16, 2880. This cosmic body is about three-quarters of a mile in diameter. And depending on how and where it hits, it could conceivably blast humanity back into the Stone Age. "This extraordinary object," remarks science writer David L. Chandler,

> will remain a major focus of small-body [i.e., asteroid and comet] research for a long time. . . . The process of devising a plan, and carrying out the first rescue of our world from a devastating blow from above, could be a project that prods human consciousness for much of the millennium to come.[55]

Trying to Prevent Doomsday

Astronomers and other scientists agree that the threat of cosmic bombardment is real and that steps need to be taken to meet that threat. The eight-hundred-year waiting period for Asteroid 1950 DA should not lull humanity into a false sense of security, they say. Thousands of undiscovered NEAs exist, new comets enter the inner solar system on a regular basis, and one or more of these objects could suddenly emerge as a planet killer at any time. "The only way to beat the odds," asserts David Levy, codiscoverer of Comet Shoemaker-Levy 9, "is to locate physically every possible asteroid or comet that could pose a threat to the Earth."[56]

Some small-scale attempts to find and calculate the orbits of potentially dangerous asteroids and comets were launched in the 1970s and 1980s in southern California. One was the Planet-Crossing Asteroid Survey (PCAS); another was the Palomar Asteroid and Comet Survey (PACS). Both were conceived and guided by the late Eugene Shoemaker, the other codiscoverer of the comet that struck Jupiter. These

Searching for Planet Killers

In this excerpt from an article in the February 2002 issue of *Astronomy*, NASA astrobiologist David Morrison summarizes the Spaceguard Survey and its goals.

The Spaceguard Survey is an international search for potentially threatening asteroids. It's named after the similar . . . search proposed by author Arthur C. Clarke in [his novel] *Rendezvous with Rama*. The survey uses a half-dozen specialized optical telescopes. The most successful of these efforts is operated by Grant Stokes and his colleagues at the MIT Lincoln Laboratory. Their twin telescopes, located in New Mexico, scan the sky every clear night except around the full moon, when faint asteroids cannot be detected. . . . Once a new asteroid is found, astronomers need to compute its orbit. The additional positions necessary are mostly obtained by a few dedicated amateur astronomers (many of them in Japan and Italy). The amateurs take measurements over successive weeks. Astronomers then calculate the position of each asteroid forward in time to ensure that it poses no danger of hitting Earth. NASA's goal is to find 90 percent of the near-Earth asteroids larger than 1 kilometer in diameter by 2009.

programs found large numbers of asteroids and comets before shutting down in 1994.

Fortunately, though, some other ambitious programs began in the 1990s. One, the Spacewatch Camera, which operates at the observatory on Kitt Peak in Arizona, finds hundreds of new asteroids each year, about thirty of them NEAs. Another program, dubbed Near-Earth Asteroid Tracking (NEAT), is centered on the summit of Mount Haleakala on Maui, Hawaii. NEAT found four NEAs in its first day of operation alone and usually discovers up to fifty per month. Still another promising program is the Spaceguard Survey, an international program funded mainly by NASA. Its truly ambitious goal is to find 90 percent of all NEAs measuring 0.6 of a mile across or larger by 2009.

If one of these programs discovers that an object like Asteroid 1950 DA will strike Earth in the near

In this scene from Deep Impact, *people watch an asteroid zooming across the sky. It will strike the ocean and generate enormous waves.*

future, what can be done to avert catastrophe? In a number of popular movies dealing with this subject, including *Armageddon* and *Deep Impact*, scientists plant nuclear bombs on the object in an attempt to blow it up. However, in most situations such an approach may cause more harm than good. Shattering the intruder will turn it into a mass of fragments, most of which will remain on a collision course with Earth. And hundreds or thousands of smaller impacts spread out over the planet's surface might be almost as destructive as one large impact.

Most scientists agree that a more prudent approach would be to push a threatening asteroid or comet into a different orbit, one that takes it away from Earth. One of the first steps in such an endeavor, says Levy,

> involves launching a reconnaissance spacecraft to study the asteroid, [to] determine whether it is

made of soft stone or solid iron and plant a transponder [tracking device] on its surface. Signals from that device would then allow us to track the asteroid accurately as it soars through space. . . . The next step, moving the asteroid, is most efficiently done at . . . the place in its path closest to the sun. At that moment . . . a nuclear warhead exploding near [not on or in] the asteroid would change the path by a small amount. . . . A few years later . . . a second shot would add to the change. By now, the asteroid should be in a new orbit that would miss the Earth. Doomsday [would] thus [be] averted.[57]

There is no way to know for sure if doomsday will ever be prevented in this manner. Perhaps humanity will someday succeed in mounting a foolproof planetary defense system that will keep it safe from bombardment from space. On the other hand, maybe global governments will not take the threat seriously enough until it is too late, and humanity will become extinct. Either way, science's fairly recent discovery of what comets and asteroids are and what they can do to the planet forces people to confront a sobering realization: Human civilization is a fragile entity existing always at the mercy of frightening cosmic forces. As Verschuur puts it, "If there is one thing the study of . . . comets and asteroids has given me, it is a profounder sense of the nature of life on Earth, our place in space."[58]

Notes

Introduction: Mountains in the Sky

1. Curtis Peebles, *Asteroids: A History*. Washington, DC: Smithsonian Institution, 2000, p. 1.
2. Quoted in Carl Sagan and Ann Druyan, *Comet*. 1985. Reprint: New York: Random House, 1997, p. 19.
3. William Shakespeare, *Julius Caesar*, act 2, scene 2, lines 30–31.
4. Plutarch, *Life of Caesar*, in *Fall of the Roman Republic: Six Lives by Plutarch*, trans. Rex Warner. New York: Penguin Books, 1972, p. 309.
5. Seneca, *Natural Questions*, trans. John Clark. London: Macmillan, 1910, pp. 275–77.
6. Quoted in Gerrit L. Verschuur, *Impact: The Threat of Comets and Asteroids*. New York: Oxford University Press, 1996, p. 55.
7. Quoted in William S. Weed, "Chasing a Comet," *Astronomy*, September 2001, p. 35.

Chapter 1: Comets Demystified, Asteroids Discovered

8. Quoted in Sagan and Druyan, *Comet*, p. 29.
9. Sagan and Druyan, *Comet*, pp. 31–32.
10. Quoted in Paul R. Weissman, "Cometary Reservoirs," in J. Kelly Beatty et al., *The New Solar System*. Cambridge, England: Cambridge University Press, 1999, pp. 59–60.
11. Quoted in Eugene MacPike, ed., *Correspondence and Papers of Edmund Halley*. Oxford, England: Clarendon Press, 1932, p. 67.
12. Quoted in Peebles, *Asteroids*, p. 5.
13. Quoted in Peebles, *Asteroids*, p. 7.
14. Quoted in Peebles, *Asteroids*, pp. 9–10.
15. Quoted in Peebles, *Asteroids*, p. 28.

Chapter 2: How Asteroids and Comets Formed

16. John K. Davies, *Beyond Pluto: Exploring the Outer Limits of the Solar System*. Cambridge, England: Cambridge University Press, 2001, p. 11.
17. Peebles, *Asteroids*, pp. 40–41.
18. Clark R. Chapman, "Asteroids," in Beatty et al., *New Solar System*, pp. 339–40.
19. John A. Wood, "Origin of the Solar System," in Beatty et al., *New Solar System*, p. 19.
20. Davies, *Beyond Pluto*, pp. 13–14.
21. David H. Levy, *Comets: Creators and Destroyers*. New York: Simon and Schuster, 1998, p. 25.
22. Weissman, "Cometary Reservoirs," p. 62.

Chapter 3: Vital Statistics of Asteroids and Comets

23. Levy, *Comets*, p. 19.
24. William K. Hartmann, *Moons and Planets*. Pacific Grove, CA: Brooks Cole, 1998, p. 201.
25. Peebles, *Asteroids*, p. 38.
26. Chapman, "Asteroids," p. 347.
27. Quoted in Weed, "Chasing a Comet," p. 34.
28. Quoted in Weed, "Chasing a Comet," p. 35.
29. John C. Brandt, "Comets," in Beatty et al., *New Solar System*, pp. 329–30.
30. Davies, *Beyond Pluto*, p. 19.
31. Quoted in Maggie Mckee, "Comets Split Far from Sun," *Astronomy*, December 2002, p. 30.
32. Brandt, "Comets," p. 335.

Chapter 4: Voyages to the Comets and Asteroids

33. Peebles, *Asteroids*, p. 100.
34. Peebles, *Asteroids*, p. 109.
35. Quoted in Peebles, *Asteroids*, p. 114.
36. Quoted in Robert Zimmerman, "NEAR-Shoemaker Scores a Touchdown," *Astronomy*, May 2001, p. 20.
37. Daniel D. Durda, "Stepping Stones to Mars," *Astronomy*, August 2001, p. 48.
38. Weed, "Chasing a Comet," p. 34.

39. Brandt, "Comets," p. 324.
40. Quoted in Richard Talcott, "Comet Borrelly's Dark Nature," *Astronomy*, April 2002, p. 44.

Chapter 5: How Humans Will Mine Asteroids and Comets

41. John S. Lewis, *Mining the Sky: Untold Riches from the Asteroids, Comets, and Planets.* Cambridge, MA: Perseus, 1997, p. 186.
42. Lewis, *Mining the Sky*, p. 194.
43. Hartmann, *Moons and Planets*, p. 211.
44. Minor Planet Center, Smithsonian Astrophysical Observatory, "Asteroids Near Earth: Retrieval for Materials Utilization," June 2003, p. 2. www.permanent.com.
45. Durda, "Stepping Stones to Mars," p. 46.
46. Minor Planet Center, "Asteroids Near Earth," p. 3.
47. Minor Planet Center, "Asteroids Near Earth," p. 16.
48. Durda, "Stepping Stones to Mars," p. 47.
49. Minor Planet Center, "Asteroids Near Earth," p. 3.

Chapter 6: When Comets and Asteroids Strike Earth

50. Verschuur, *Impact*, p. 6.
51. Alan E. Rubin, *Disturbing the Solar System: Impacts, Close Encounters, and Coming Attractions*, Princeton, NJ: Princeton University Press, 2002, pp. 156–57.
52. Verschuur, *Impact*, pp. 7–8.
53. Quoted in Hartmann, *Moons and Planets*, p. 215.
54. John S. Lewis, *Rain of Iron and Ice: The Very Real Threat of Comet and Asteroid Bombardment.* Reading, MA: Addison-Wesley, 1996, p. 151.
55. David L. Chandler, "Asteroid for the Millennium," *Astronomy*, December 2002, p. 46.
56. Levy, *Comets*, p. 157.
57. Levy, *Comets*, pp. 155–56.
58. Verschuur, *Impact*, p. 221.

Glossary

accretion: A process in which clumps of material stick together, forming a larger clump.

asteroid: "Starlike object"; a small stony or metallic body orbiting the Sun.

asteroid belt: A region lying between the orbits of the planets Mars and Jupiter, where most of the asteroids are located.

astronomical unit (AU): The distance from Earth to the Sun, about 93 million miles.

clathrates: Mixtures of carbon dioxide, sulfur dioxide, and water ice.

compound asteroid: An asteroid consisting of two smaller asteroids held together by their mutual gravities.

gravity: A force exerted by an object that attracts other objects. The pull of Earth's gravity keeps rocks, trees, people, and houses from floating away into space and holds the Moon in orbit around Earth.

hydrates: Mixtures in which water molecules are trapped within crystals of other substances.

impact crater: A hole in the ground created by the collision of an asteroid or comet from space.

K-T event: The impact of a large comet or asteroid that generated a mass extinction of life, including the dinosaurs, about 65 million years ago. The event ended the Cretaceous era and initiated the Tertiary era.

Kuiper Belt: A region lying beyond the orbit of the planet Neptune that contains millions of comets, along with some asteroids.

long-period comets: Comets that originate in the Oort Cloud, move into the inner solar system, and then return to the Oort Cloud.

mass: The total amount of matter contained in an object.

meteors: Small pieces of old, disintegrated asteroids and comets.

near-Earth asteroids (NEAs): Asteroids that come near or cross Earth's orbit.

nebula: A gaseous cloud or a cloudlike phenomenon.

Oort Cloud: A vast shell of comets (and a few asteroids) located on the outer fringes of the solar system.

orbit: To move around something, or the path taken by a planet, comet, or asteroid around a star (or a moon around a planet).

parallax: The apparent movement of an object against a distant background when the object is seen from two different vantage points.

planet: A large solid or gaseous object orbiting the Sun or another star.

planetesimals: Small objects that orbit a young star and combine to form planets, moons, asteroids, and comets.

rotate: To spin around a central axis.

short-period comets: Comets that are captured by the gravities of the planets and thereafter orbit within the planetary region.

silicates: Hard minerals made up of a mixture of silicon and oxygen compounds.

solar nebula hypothesis (or nebular hypothesis): The accepted theory that the Sun and its family condensed out of a large cloud of gases and dust.

solar system: The Sun, or a star, and all of the objects that orbit it.

spherical: Round like a ball.

stellar: Having to do with stars.

sublimation: The process in which a solid turns directly into a gas, skipping the liquid stage.

Titius-Bode Law: A mathematical pattern in which, moving outward from the Sun, each planet orbits at about one-and-a-half to two times the distance as the one before it.

tsunami: A large sea wave generated by an underwater earthquake or an oceanic impact of a comet or asteroid.

vaporize: To change into a vapor.

volatiles: Water and other light substances that easily vaporize.

For Further Reading

Books

Mary A. Barnes and Kathleen Duey, *The Ultimate Asteroid Book: The Inside Story on the Threat from the Skies*. New York: Aladdin Paperbacks, 1998. An excellent introduction to asteroids and how they pose a potential threat to Earth.

Pam Beasant, *1000 Facts About Space*. New York: Kingfisher Books, 1992. An informative collection of basic facts about the stars, planets, asteroids, and other heavenly bodies.

Samantha Bonar, *Asteroids*. Danbury, CT: Franklin Watts, 2000. A general overview of asteroids, highlighted by numerous photos.

———, *Comets*. Danbury, CT: Franklin Watts, 1998. A well-written introduction to comets and the manner in which scientists determined their true identity.

Nigel Henbest, *DK Space Encyclopedia*. London: Dorling Kindersley, 1999. This beautifully mounted and critically acclaimed book is the best general source available for grade-school readers about the wonders of space.

Douglas Henderson, *Asteroid Impact*. New York: Dial Books, 2000. A very handsomely illustrated volume that also contains much useful information about asteroids and how some of them have struck Earth.

Robin Kerrod, *Asteroids, Comets, and Meteors*. Minneapolis: Lerner, 2003. This well-written book covers a wide range of facts about the remnants of the formation of the solar system. Highly recommended.

Internet Sources

NASA, "National Space Science Data Center (NSSDC) Photo

Gallery: Asteroids." http://nssdc.gsfc.nasa.gov/photo_gallery. Excellent collection of photos and facts about major asteroids.

———, "National Space Science Data Center (NSSDC) Photo Gallery: Comets." http://nssdc.gsfc.nasa.gov/photo_gallery. Another fine collection of pictures and information, this one about comets.

———, "NEAR-Shoemaker: Near Earth Asteroid Rendezvous." http://nssdc.gsfc.nasa.gov/planetary/near.html. The story of the successful touchdown of a spacecraft on the asteroid Eros on February 12, 2001.

Major Works Consulted

Patricia Barnes-Svarney, *Asteroid: Earth Destroyer or New Frontier?* New York: Plenum, 1996. An excellent overview of the potential of asteroids to strike Earth, causing catastrophes, and to be exploited by humanity for their valuable metals and other resources.

J. Kelly Beatty et al., *The New Solar System.* Cambridge, England: Cambridge University Press, 1999. One of the best available general guides to ongoing knowledge and discoveries in planetary science, including valuable information about asteroids and comets.

John K. Davies, *Beyond Pluto: Exploring the Outer Limits of the Solar System.* Cambridge, England: Cambridge University Press, 2001. An absorbing study of present information and theories regarding the Kuiper Belt and Oort Cloud and other aspects of the outer solar system.

William K. Hartmann, *Moons and Planets.* Pacific Grove, CA: Brooks Cole, 1998. Very well-written and useful general overview of the solar system, including some detailed information about comets, asteroids, and meteors.

David H. Levy, *Comets: Creators and Destroyers.* New York: Simon and Schuster, 1998. As Levy explains in this well-informed volume, comets probably brought much of Earth's carbon and water, both of which are essential for the generation of life.

John S. Lewis, *Mining the Sky: Untold Riches from the Asteroids, Comets, and Planets.* Cambridge, MA: Perseus, 1997. Excellent, thought-provoking overview of humans mining the solar system in the twenty-first century and beyond. Highly recommended.

———, *Rain of Iron and Ice: The Very Real Threat of Comet and Asteroid Bombardment.* Reading, MA: Addison-Wesley, 1996.

Another fine volume by Lewis, this one focuses on the threat posed by asteroids and comets striking Earth.

Curtis Peebles, *Asteroids: A History.* Washington, DC: Smithsonian Institution, 2000. Peebles, a noted aerospace historian, delivers a fascinating overview of how human beings discovered and learned about asteroids.

James L. Powell, *Night Comes to the Cretaceous: Comets, Craters, Controversy, and the Last Days of the Dinosaurs.* New York: Harcourt Brace, 1998. The most comprehensive summary of the debate about dinosaur extinction. Powell presents the evidence gathered so far showing that an asteroid or comet impacted Earth 65 million years ago, causing a major mass extinction. Highly recommended.

Alan E. Rubin, *Disturbing the Solar System: Impacts, Close Encounters, and Coming Attractions.* Princeton, NJ: Princeton University Press, 2002. An eclectic but highly informative book about the known celestial objects, as well as the mysteries of outer space.

Carl Sagan and Ann Druyan, *Comet.* 1985. Reprint: New York: Random House, 1997. A massive, very informative study of the folklore, discovery, origins, composition, orbits, and potential dangers of comets. Highly recommended.

William Sheehan, *Worlds in the Sky: Planetary Discovery from the Earliest Times Through Voyager and Magellan.* Tucson: University of Arizona Press, 1992. The author provides detailed information about how human beings discovered or came to understand the workings of asteroids, comets, and other cosmic bodies.

Gerrit L. Verschuur, *Impact: The Threat of Comets and Asteroids.* New York: Oxford University Press, 1996. A well-researched and well-written examination of the real threat of extraterrestrial bombardment of Earth.

David K. Yeomans, *Comets: A Chronological History of Observation, Science, Myth, and Folklore.* New York: John Wiley, 1991. Explains why people used to fear comets and how science showed that these celestial objects are remnants of the formation of the solar system.

Additional Works Consulted

Books

Walter Alvarez, *T. Rex and the Crater of Doom.* Princeton, NJ: Princeton University Press, 1997.

Thomas T. Arny, *Explorations: An Introduction to Astronomy.* New York: McGraw-Hill, 2001.

Isaac Asimov, *Asimov's Guide to Halley's Comet.* New York: Walker, 1985.

———, *A Choice of Catastrophes.* New York: Simon and Schuster, 1979.

———, *Counting the Eons.* New York: Avon, 1983.

———, *Did Comets Kill the Dinosaurs?* Milwaukee, WI: Gareth Stevens, 1988.

———, *From Earth to Heaven.* New York: Avon, 1966.

Commission on Planetary and Lunar Exploration, *Exploring the Trans-Neptunian Solar System.* Washington, DC: National Academy Press, 1998.

Jacques Crovisier et al. *Comet Science: The Study of Remnants from the Birth of the Solar System.* Cambridge, England: Cambridge University Press, 2000.

Clifford J. Cunningham, *The First Asteroid: Ceres, 1801–2001.* Surfside, FL: Star Lab, 2001.

———, *Introduction to Asteroids: The Next Frontier.* Richmond, VA: Willman-Bell, 1988.

Eugene MacPike, ed., *Correspondence and Papers of Edmund Halley.* Oxford, England: Clarendon Press, 1932.

Plutarch, *Life of Caesar*. In *Fall of the Roman Republic: Six Lives by Plutarch*. Trans. Rex Warner. New York: Penguin Books, 1972.

Seneca, *Natural Questions*. Trans. John Clark. London: Macmillan, 1910.

Leon Silver and P.H. Schultz, eds., *Geological Implications of Impacts of Large Asteroids and Comets on the Earth*. Boulder, CO: Geological Society of America, 1982.

Periodicals

Louis W. Alvarez, Walter Alvarez et al., "Extraterrestrial Cause for the Cretaceous-Tertiary Extinction," *Science*, vol. 208, 1980.

Walter Alvarez and Frank Asaro, "An Extraterrestrial Impact," *Scientific American*, vol. 263, 1990.

Michael J. Benton, "Scientific Methodologies in Collision: The History of the Study of the Extinction of the Dinosaurs," *Evolutionary Biology*, vol. 24, 1990.

David L. Chandler, "Asteroid for the Millennium," *Astronomy*, December 2002.

C.R. Chapman, "Impacts on Earth by Asteroids and Comets: Assessing the Hazard," *Nature*, vol. 367, 1994.

Clifford J. Cunningham, "Giuseppe Piazzi and the Missing Planet," *Sky and Telescope*, September 1992.

Daniel D. Durda, "Stepping Stones to Mars," *Astronomy*, August 2001.

Pamela L. Gay, "Giant Iceball Found Beyond Pluto," *Astronomy*, January 2003.

David H. Levy, Eugene M. Shoemaker et al., "Comet Shoemaker-Levy 9 Meets Jupiter," *Scientific American*, vol. 273, 1995.

J.X. Luu and D.C. Jewitt, "The Kuiper Belt," *Scientific American*, May 1996.

Maggie Mckee, "Comets Split Far from Sun," *Astronomy*, December 2002.

Virginia Morell, "How Lethal Was the K-T Impact?" *Science*, September 17, 1993.

David Morrison, "Target Earth," *Astronomy*, February 2002.

J.H. Oort, "The Structure of the Cloud of Comets Surrounding the Solar System, and a Hypothesis Concerning Its Origin," *Bulletin of the Astronomical Institutes of the Netherlands 11*, vol. 91, 1950.

Tom Polakis, "The Comet Seekers," *Astronomy*, January 2003.

Carol Ryback, "Tearing Apart Asteroid Families," *Astronomy*, March 2002.

William Schomaker, "Big Fish in the Kuiper Belt?" *Astronomy*, October 2001.

——, "Space Rocks Bridge the Gap," *Astronomy*, June 2001.

——, "A Trim New Look for the Oort Cloud," *Astronomy*, June 2001.

Richard Talcott, "Comet Borrelly's Dark Nature," *Astronomy*, April 2002.

William S. Weed, "Chasing a Comet," *Astronomy*, September 2001.

Paul R. Weissman, "The Oort Cloud," *Nature*, April 1990.

Fred Whipple, "The Black Heart of Halley's Comet," *Sky and Telescope*, vol. 73, 1987.

Robert Zimmerman, "NEAR-Shoemaker Scores a Touchdown," *Astronomy*, May 2001.

Internet Sources

Bill Arnett, "Asteroids," May 2003. www.seds.org/billa/tnp/asteroids.html. Good general overview of asteroid types and locations.

Kevin Bonsor, "How Asteroid Mining Will Work," June 2003. www.science.howstuffworks.com/asteroid-mining.htm. Introduces the concept of asteroid mining and provides links to "Valuable Asteroid Resources" and "Extraction and Processing."

Mark Kilner, "Mining Asteroids," April 2001. www.kilnet.free serve.co.uk/astmine.htm. A brief synopsis of the value of mining asteroids.

Minor Planet Center, Smithsonian Astrophysical Observatory, "Asteroids Near Earth: Retrieval for Materials Utilization," June 2003. www.permanent.com. A large, very useful source explaining the compositions of asteroids and details about how they will likely be mined and otherwise exploited.

NASA, "Asteroids," July 2001. http://nssdc.gsfc.nasa.gov/planetary/text/asteroids.txt. Overview of asteroids, concentrating most on near-Earth asteroids.

———, "Astronomers Discover a Moon Orbiting an Asteroid," October 6, 1999. http://nssdc.gsfc.nasa.gov/planetary/news. Information about a satellite asteroid revolving around the asteroid Eugenia.

———, "Dawn," March 2002. http://nssdc.gsfc.nasa.gov/database/MasterCatalog?sc=DAWN. Overview of NASA plans to rendezvous with the asteroids Vesta and Ceres in 2006.

———, "Deep Impact," April 2003. http://nssdc.gsfc.nasa.gov/database/MasterCatalog?sc=DEEPIMP. Tells about the NASA mission to rendezvous with Comet P/Tempel in 2004.

———, "NEAR Shoemaker Makes Historic Touchdown on Asteroid Eros," February 2001. http://nssdc.gsfc.nasa.gov/planetary/text/near_pr_20010212.txt. Bulletin announcing NASA's landing of a spacecraft on Eros.

———, "New Kuiper Belt Object Discovered, Possibly Larger than Ceres," December 2000. http://cfa-www.harvard.edu. Bulletin about a large object, either an asteroid or a giant comet, found in the Kuiper Belt.

Smithsonian Astrophysical Observatory, "One-Mile-Wide Asteroid to Pass Close to the Earth in 2028," June 2003. http://cfa-www.harvard.edu/iau/pressinfo. Information about the close approach of Asteroid 1997XF in October 2028.

Index

Picture Credits

About the Author

In addition to his acclaimed volumes on ancient civilizations, historian Don Nardo has published several studies of modern scientific discoveries and phenomena. Among these are *Black Holes; Extraterrestrial Life; The Extinction of the Dinosaurs; Cloning;* volumes about Pluto, Neptune, and the Moon; and a biography of the noted scientist Charles Darwin. Mr. Nardo lives with his wife, Christine, in Massachusetts.